FUNDAMENTALISM

AND THE CHURCH OF GOD

Fundamentalism and the Church of God

GABRIEL HEBERT, D.D.

Society of the Sacred Mission
St Michael's, Crafers
South Australia

SCM PRESS LTD
56 BLOOMSBURY STREET
LONDON

First published June 1957

PRINTED IN GREAT BRITAIN BY
THE BOWERING PRESS, PLYMOUTH

Contents

5

Preface

THE things which an author commonly says in a Preface have been mostly said in the first chapter of this book and in the brief Postscript at the end. In the first chapter I have explained the line of approach which I have taken; why it is that I have refrained so far as possible from calling 'fundamentalists' by a name which they do not use of themselves, and have tried to avoid the tone of a counsel for the prosecution and to take the line that Christians ought to take in controversy with one another.

My acknowledgements are due to two conservative evangelical friends here in Australia, both Anglicans, who have helped me much by the loan of books and in discussion; to Dr S. P. Hebart, of the (Lutheran) Immanuel Seminary in Adelaide for an especially valuable loan of books; to Dr Hermann Sasse, also of Immanuel Seminary, for permission to quote from an article of his, and to summarize part of the argument of his article; to the Rev. R. Swanton, for permission to make the quotation from the *Reformed Theological Review* in which the article appeared; to the Bishop of Gothenburg in Sweden, whom I first knew as an undergraduate at Uppsala twenty-seven years ago, for his generous permission to make a digest of part of one of his books; to Sir J. F. Wolfenden, Vice-Chancellor of Reading University, for sending me the text of part of a lecture given by him; to the editor of *The Advertiser*, Adelaide, for two quotations; to Messrs Angus and Robertson, Sydney, for two quotations; and finally to the Brethren of my Community for much help, encouragement and criticism in the writing of this book.

GABRIEL HEBERT, S.S.M.

ST MICHAEL'S HOUSE,
CRAFERS, SOUTH AUSTRALIA
May 1956

I

The Aim of this Book

WHAT is Fundamentalism? It is described in the *Oxford English Dictionary* (Supplement, 1933) as 'a religious movement which became active among various Protestant bodies in the United States after the war of 1914–18, based on strict adherence to traditional orthodox tenets (e.g. the literal inerrancy of Scripture) held to be fundamental to the Christian faith: opposed to *liberalism* and *modernism*.' The *Concise Oxford Dictionary* attempts a definition: 'the maintenance, in opposition to modernism, of traditional orthodox beliefs such as the inerrancy of Scripture and literal acceptance of the creeds as fundamentals of Protestant Christianity.'

The word had certainly come into use in the United States by the year 1920. In *The Christian Graduate* (I.V.F., London) for March 1955, Dr Douglas Johnson gives an account of its origin, and says that it was probably coined by the editor of the New York *Watchman-Examiner*, who in his editorial for July 1st, 1920 describes as 'fundamentalists' those 'who mean to do battle royal for the fundamentals'. As he goes on to show, the term 'the fundamentals' had been made familiar by a series of booklets which had been issued between 1909 and 1915. He gives an interesting short summary of these, and I shall give in Chapter II an account of them in the context in which they appeared.

For a time the term 'Fundamentalism' seems to have been accepted and used as a title of honour by those who stood for it. But before long the indiscreet action of some of its supporters, in 'trials for heresy, resolutions to assemblies of the churches, and somewhat bitter articles in the press' (*The Christian Graduate*, p. 25) brought it into disrepute; and now it seems to be used only by critics and opponents. In the correspondence in *The*

Times on Fundamentalism in August 1955, the Rev. J. R. W. Stott, rector of All Souls', Langham Place, London W., expresses his dislike of it as a word which has become 'almost a symbol for obscurantism, and is generally used as a term of opprobrium. It appears to describe the bigoted rejection of all biblical criticism, a mechanical view of inspiration, and an excessively literalist interpretation of Scripture.'[1] He wishes to be called a 'conservative evangelical'; Dr Johnson says the same.

It is with conservative evangelicals in the Church of England and other churches, and with the Inter-Varsity Fellowship of Evangelical Unions, that this book is to be specially concerned. It will be therefore only common courtesy on my part to refrain from calling them by a name which they dislike and repudiate. I can however fittingly use it in its strict sense, of the original Fundamentalists who were responsible for the booklets entitled 'The Fundamentals'. For its use in a number of quotations which I shall make I am not responsible. But it is almost impossible to avoid it altogether; when however I use it as a general term, I shall always have in mind the evil meaning which it bears for Mr Stott, to whom it is 'a term of opprobrium'.

My second chapter, as I have said, will be occupied with the original Fundamentalists and the situation in which they arose; like this first chapter, it will be of an introductory character.

After this there will be five chapters, III to VII, about the interpretation of Scripture and the problems raised by the word 'inerrancy'. I shall first sketch out a positive view of the Bible, with which I trust that the readers whom I have in mind will be in principle agreed. Then we shall go on to consider what we mean when we say that 'the Bible is true', and the 'truth' of our statements about God, and the 'truth' of science and of criticism; and then to review the beliefs of conservative evangelicals about these things. In all this, the real questions which we must consider lie much deeper than the mere question whether God has preserved the biblical writers from all erroneous statements. The real question is, in a phrase which I owe to a conservative evangelical friend here in Australia: 'How does the Word of

[1] Letter to *The Times*, 25th August, 1955.

God come to us in Holy Scripture, and how is this Word of God to be distinguished from the words of men?'

The Word of God is the Word which He has spoken, and still speaks. It is His Word, and calls for our entire acceptance and obedience. The words of men, spoken and written, belong to this world; and the written words of men are subject to literary and historical criticism. The Bible consists of words of men; hence there must be literary and historical criticism of the Bible. But through those words of men the Word of God has been spoken and still speaks, the Word of which it is written, 'To-day, if ye shall hear His voice, harden not your hearts.'

It follows that, in regard to this Word of God spoken through words of men, we are required to be at once humble and docile, and alert and critical. We must be critical; an entirely uncritical person would be entirely gullible, foolish and superstitious, and entirely unable to discern truth from error and good from evil. There is at the same time danger in being critical; in making our judgments both on what we call ordinary things and on what we call spiritual things, we are liable to be led into wrong judgments by the disturbing influences of our pride in our own opinions, jealousy of other people, the weight of custom and usage, or the current view of the group to which we belong. This is why, as we have all been taught, in the interpreting of the Holy Scriptures there is need of the same Spirit who inspired them to interpret them to us, and make us humble and docile to hear God's Word that is spoken in them. It would be right to say that the ideal biblical student would have to be as sharply and even daringly critical as is humanly possible, and at the same time deeply sensitive to the things of the spirit, and so far as his will goes entirely obedient to God's will.

The interpretation of the Bible is the continual task of the Church of God. Here I will quote some illuminating words of Dr Hermann Sasse:[1]

---

[1] In a new Introduction to a paper 'Sacra Scriptura', originally written in German, and published in translated form in the *Reformed Theological Review* (304 Glenferrie Road, Hawthorn, E.2, Melbourne, Victoria) Oct. 1955, pp. 65-6. Dr Sasse was formerly professor at Erlangen, and is now at Immanuel Theological Seminary, North Adelaide, South Australia.

'The quest for the authority of Holy Scripture has become one of the foremost problems for all Christendom, for Catholics and Protestants, for the churches in countries with an old Christian tradition as well as for the younger churches in the mission fields throughout the world. This fact indicates the presence of a deep crisis within Christianity itself. It is a universally accepted doctrine of all churches, with the exception of some modern Christian bodies which have more or less severed their connection with historic Christianity, that Holy Scripture is given by inspiration of God and is therefore the infallible Word of God in writing. . . .

During the last 250 years, it is true, the impact of modern historical research seemed often to endanger or even to destroy the old view, founded on the biblical statements themselves, of the Bible as being in its entirety—from cover to cover, so to speak—the inspired and infallible Word of God. In our days, however, the fight between Fundamentalism and Modernism is becoming more and more obsolete because the tacit *philosophical* presuppositions of either view have proved untenable. A Bible Movement is proceeding throughout Christendom, the deeper reason for which is that all churches are confronted with the task of finding a new theological understanding of the written Word of God. The great encyclicals on the Bible by the modern popes, such as *De sacrorum Bibliorum studiis* of 1943, or the new Latin translation of the psalms, reveal something of the amazing work which is being done in this direction by Rome. The fresh approach to a theological understanding of the Bible by Anglican and Reformed scholars, Karl Barth's Dogmatics, and the rediscovery of Luther's Christological understanding of the Bible—all this shows that the churches are beginning to realize their precarious situation, as it became manifest at Evanston and as it is keenly felt in the mission fields. How can the churches meet the challenge presented by the great religions of Asia and by the powerful political substitutes for religion in our age, unless they know what they are saying when they claim that the Bible *is* God's Word?'

Alas, it is not possible in this book to give more than very brief and summary discussions of the problems that we must raise. But at least we need to remind ourselves at the start how wide and deep the problem of biblical interpretation actually is.

The last section of this book, consisting of Chapters VIII to X, will deal with the other side of our problem. The movement which the world calls Fundamentalism believes itself to be above all a great religious revival, which sets out to proclaim the whole demand of God for man's obedience, both in the home lands and overseas in the most heathen parts of the world. Problems arise here. When people have become converted, how are they to live out their lives in the light of their conversion? Is their Christian fellowship with one another to lead to the formation of parties, groups, sects? What then is their relation to the whole Church of God, or does the true Church of God consist only of those who have been thus converted? This is the reason why the title of this book had to be 'Fundamentalism and the Church of God'.

In questions such as these it is impossible for a Christian to be a detached and 'impartial' onlooker. One must try with all one's might to see the issues honestly and truly; but one is compelled to take sides. For myself, I believe that Fundamentalism (in the evil sense) is a grave menace to the Church of God. A controversy is in fact going on between believing Christians, in which both sides hold the orthodox faith, and yet are seriously in conflict with one another. The conflict is such that they find it difficult and often impossible to worship together and work together; witness the difficulty of the relations between the Student Christian Movement and the Evangelical Unions, and the many other instances in our church life in which a similar issue comes up. This book has been called out by that controversy. It is of the first importance therefore that now at the start something should be said about the right and the wrong way to conduct a controversy. The point at which we are compelled to start is this:

It is impossible that a controversy between believing Christians should end in final disagreement; for Christ has made them one. There is in Him a Ground of Unity which lies deeper than all their differences. This unity is of God. Christ died, as St John says, that He might 'gather together in one the children of God that were scattered abroad'.[1] He came that there might be 'one Flock, one Shepherd'.[2] 'There is one body and one Spirit, even as also ye were called in one hope of your calling; one God, one faith, one baptism, one God and Father of all, who is above all and through all and in all'.[3] This theme runs through the whole New Testament, beginning with the prayer which our Lord taught us: 'Our Father'—then we are all His children and brothers to one another.

This unity is of God. The Son of God has created it by His death and resurrection. We men are all different from one another, for God has made us different; yet in Christ we are one. Because we are different, we easily find ourselves opposed to one another. The separations between Christians have in our day assumed fearful proportions; we are split by schisms into various denominations, and within the denominations there are groups and parties at variance with one another. Yet God has made us one; and the unity which He has made lies deeper than the divisions which we have made.

Therefore all controversy between Christians needs to start from the unity which God has made. The right way of controversy starts from the realization that our opponent in the controversy is our brother. I must treat my opponent as my brother in Christ. I must try to understand what are the things which the Lord has taught him and his friends, what is the way by which He has led them. His ways of worship, his ways of thinking, are different from those which I have learnt. I must try to get him to tell me. I must not do all the talking. I must try to learn what is the background of his strange views, and the questions to which he thinks that those views are the answer. Perhaps, if I am patient, he will give me the opportunity to express my views, in answer to his questions.

The wrong way of controversy is unhappily all too familiar. I set out to demonstrate that I am right and he is wrong. In

[1] John 11. 52.   [2] John 10. 16.   [3] Eph. 4. 5–6.

doing so, I state what I take to be his position; and this in itself is a most irritating thing to do, for I know how I feel when others do it to me. I prove that he is wrong; but if I seem to have won the argument, I have really lost it, for I have sent him away determined to think up all the counter-arguments which he failed to express adequately when he was arguing with me. In the discussion I have stood before him not as a brother in Christ, but as a rival and an opponent; I have not come within range of his real convictions, the things which to his mind are self-evidently true. When he says at the end, 'Here you and I differ', those words mark the fact that I have done no good, but only harm.[1]

This wrong method of controversy breathes the very spirit which divides us into parties, sects, and denominations. It embodies in itself the very essence of sectarianism, when we (whoever 'we' are) think that we of our group or party possess the whole truth, have answers to all questions, and say of ourselves, 'We at least have nothing to learn', or 'See how right we were'.

Yet there is a Ground of Unity deeper than all our differences. It consists in the fact that Christ died on the cross for the salvation of all mankind. The Ground of Unity is in the Son of God. And because the Truth of God is greater than my understanding of it, I must not speak as if I or my people were capable of grasping and expressing the whole truth, and I must endeavour to save my opponent from taking up a similar false position. The wrong way of controversy has the evil effect of making it impossible for those who ought to be learning from one another to do so. The right way of controversy does make it possible for the differences of view to be analyzed, for misunderstandings on both sides to be cleared up, and for both sides to learn from one another. The aim of it is to seek that Unity in which those who confess God's holy Name come to agree in the truth of His holy Word, and live in unity, and godly love.

---

[1] For some entirely admirable remarks on the art of controversy, see John Lawrence's editorial in *The Christian Newsletter*, Jan., 1954, 'On Talking with other Christians'.

It is not, indeed, that the differences between us are unimportant. There is no answer to any real problem in that easy exhortation to be charitable which assumes that the differences between our various insights into truth do not matter, and that toleration at the expense of truth is a Christian virtue. The differences between us are real, on our human level; we, being human, must fight our way through them on that level. There was much that was very wrong in the persecutions of the Reformation period; but at least our forefathers did care about what they believed to be true. Even schism, it may be, is better than a pretence of agreement where no agreement exists, or than an imposed uniformity.

The subject of the Ground of Unity is to be dealt with in Chapter IX. But it was necessary to say this much at the start, because the whole method of the book depends upon it. My endeavour throughout will be to follow the right way of controversy and avoid the wrong way. But it is not easy, because a book is necessarily a monologue and not a dialogue: I shall be compelled to state other people's opinions for them, and perhaps they will think that I am unfair to them. But I will try not to score unfair points. And also it is not easy, because in this particular controversy there exists much party-spirit, much alienation of the opposing sides from one another, much refusal to work together, much mutual denunciation; there are rival orthodoxies confronting each other, and the possibility of further ecclesiastical schism.

But those who believe that God has in Christ reconciled the world to Himself can never accept final disagreement as the end of any controversy. We differ; but the Lord judges between us, and judges *us*, both now and in the Day of His final Judgment. He is also the Reconciler, now, while there is yet time.

II

The Fundamentals

WHEN the name 'Fundamentalist' was first given, it was intended to recall a series of booklets entitled 'The Fundamentals', which began to appear in 1909; they were in paper covers, and contained 128 pages each; they were issued by the Testimony Publishing Company (not inc.), Chicago, Ill., and were distributed free of charge with the 'compliments of two Christian laymen' to 'every pastor, evangelist, missionary, theological professor, theological student, Sunday-school superintendent, Y.M.C.A. and Y.W.C.A. secretary, in the English-speaking world, so far as the addresses of all these can be obtained.' Twelve numbers were issued, between 1909 and 1915, and the total number of booklets thus distributed was about three million.[1]

The first volume contained seven papers, with the following titles: 'The Virgin Birth of Christ', by Professor James Orr of the United Free Church College, Glasgow (an excellent and scholarly apologetic treatise); 'The Deity of Christ', by Professor B. B. Warfield, of Princeton Theological Seminary, Princeton, New Jersey (excellent); 'The Purpose of the Incarnation', by G. Campbell Morgan, Westminster Chapel, London ('to reveal God; to take away sins; to destroy the works of the devil; to prepare for His second Advent'); 'The Personality and Deity of the Holy Spirit', by R. A. Torrey (good); 'The Proof of the Living God', by A. T. Pierson ('as found in the prayer-life of George Muller of Bristol'); 'The History of the Higher Criticism', by Canon Dyson Hague, of London, Ontario ('what the Conservative school oppose is not Biblical Criticism as such, but Biblical Criticism by rationalists'); and finally 'A Personal Testimony' by an eminent physician and surgeon, Dr Howard Kelly of Baltimore, Maryland.

[1] This information is taken from the booklets themselves.

This first booklet set a high standard. It would be too much to say that this standard was fully maintained in all the later numbers; but at least it marked out the line which they followed. It might seem that the paper of 'The Proof of the Living God' was not quite worthy of its place in so distinguished a series, owing to the limitation of its scope; but this fault, if it was a fault, was made good later. In Vol. VI there is an admirable paper by Thomas Whitelaw, of Kilmarnock, Scotland, on 'Is there a God?', which sets itself to grapple seriously with the actual positions taken up by atheistic materialism; perhaps the one defect is a failure (more pardonable then than it would be now) to recognize the provisional character of scientific hypotheses, and an attempt to discredit the work of the scientists on this ground. Another paper, on 'The Knowledge of God', by David James Burrell of New York, in Vol. VIII, deals with the traditional arguments of Natural Theology for the existence of God, and shows that they fall short as demonstrations, and that it is only through revelation that God can be really known.

The subjects dealt with in these booklets may be thus classified:

(i) *'The Fundamentals' of the Faith.* We have seen already how seriously this subject is dealt with. The booklets contain many expositions of the orthodox Christian faith, in the traditional 'evangelical' manner; these include the Atonement ('At-one-ment by Propitiation'), the reality of Hell ('What Christ teaches concerning Future Retribution'), the Second Advent. But 'The True Church', by 'the late Bishop Ryle'[1] in Vol. IX, sets forth a doctrine of a wholly Invisible Church.

(ii) *A series of attacks on the current Biblical Criticism*, which, as we shall see in a moment, was often pantheistic in theology and treated the Bible chiefly as the record of a remarkable religious development. The paper in Vol. I on Biblical Criticism is discriminating, and does not condemn the righteous with the ungodly among the critics. Other titles are 'Fallacies of Higher

---

[1] This is not H. E. Ryle, Bishop of Winchester, who lived till 1925, but his father J. C. Ryle, who was a prominent evangelical leader and first Bishop of Liverpool; he died in 1900.

Criticism', 'My personal experience of Higher Criticism'. There are many papers on the Bible from the conservative point of view: on Inspiration, on 'The early narratives of Genesis', 'The Mosaic Authorship of the Pentateuch', 'One Isaiah', 'Christ and Criticism', 'Prophecy Fulfilled: a potent Argument for the Bible'.

(iii) A few papers deal with *scientific theories*, in view of the threat which these then seemed to present to the doctrine of the Creation: 'The Decadence of Darwinism', 'Evolutionism in the Pulpit', 'The Passing of Evolution'.

(iv) There are also some *attacks on modern heresies*: 'Mormonism, its origin, characteristics and doctrines'; 'Millennial Dawn: a Counterfeit of Christianity'; 'Eddyism, commonly called Christian Science'; 'Spiritualism'. There are two on the Roman Church, 'Romanism: is it Christianity?', and 'Rome, the Antagonist of the Nation'.

(v) There are a number of *personal testimonies* and papers on *personal religion*:, such as 'The Divine Efficacy of Prayer', 'Consecration', 'Salvation by Grace'.

(vi) There are several papers on *missions throughout the world*, and on *evangelism*. To Evangelism the last volume (XII) is devoted. The titles are: 'Doctrines that must be emphasized in successful Evangelism', 'Pastoral and Personal Evangelism; or, Winning men to Christ one by one', 'The Sunday School's true Evangelism', 'Foreign Missions, or, World-wide Evangelism', 'What missionary motives should prevail?', 'The Place of Prayer in Evangelism', and 'The Church and Socialism'.

In all this, there are clearly two strands; one is the 'battle royal for the fundamentals', for the Gospel of God itself, and the other is the rejection of scientific and critical-historical theories which appeared to be inconsistent with faith in God's revelation. We must now sketch out briefly the dangers which these 'Fundamentalists' discerned in the work partly of natural scientists and anthropologists, but still more in that of the Liberal theologians, who seemed to them to be betraying that Faith of which they were accredited teachers, and endorsing the suspicion in the popular mind that the Bible was 'a fallen oracle'.[1] We shall try later, in chapter VI, to assess the positive truths for which, with all their faults, the Liberal critics were standing.

The main points are these:

(a) Astronomy, geology and biology seemed to be calling in question the truth of the account of the creation in Genesis, and endangering the belief in God as the Creator of heaven and earth.

(b) The account of the Fall of Man in Genesis 2 and 3 was being treated as a piece of primitive and childish folklore; Adam and Eve never existed.

(c) The new study of Comparative Religion, as applied to the religions of the ancient Middle East, showed striking parallels with the Old Testament, and the influence of pagan religious ideas could be traced in it in many places.

(d) The Old Testament books were analysed into sources; thus for instance the main sources of the five books of the Pentateuch were labelled J, E, D, and P. The last of these was to be dated during and after the Exile, and the Pentateuch could not have been written by Moses.

(e) With this went a theology which interpreted the Bible in evolutionary terms, in the light of the nineteenth-century belief in Progress. The Bible reflected the moral and religious development of a 'nation with a genius for religion'; it took its place in the general evolution of the world-religions. In the earlier part of the biblical history, comment was freely made on 'the ferocity of Yahweh', as a belief that was later outgrown. It was not till the writing prophets that Monotheism emerged; and it was in the prophets chiefly that the religiously valuable parts of the Old Testament were to be found. The story of the Exodus was mainly legendary, and the faith that God had then called Israel to be His people and made His Covenant with them was a later prophetic invention.

(f) The New Testament likewise came under criticism. Our

---

[1] A valuable contemporary document is Orr, *Revelation and Inspiration* (Duckworth, 1910), a book of much wisdom and insight. Chaps. I and II contain his criticism of Ewald, Bousset, and other Liberal leaders.

Lord was regarded as above all the proclaimer of ultimate religious truths; in Harnack's lectures on *Das Wesen des Christentums,* delivered in Berlin in 1899–1900 (E.T. *What is Christianity?,* 1901) these were summed up as the Fatherhood of God, the Brotherhood of Man, and the Infinite Value of the Individual Soul. This was the original Gospel; and it was first Paul who perverted this sunny Galilean Gospel into a message of salvation from sin, and initiated the degradation of the original Christianity into the later Catholicism.

(g) With this went a 'reduced Christology'. If this was the original Gospel proclamation, it was really irrelevant whether or no Jesus believed Himself to be the Messiah; other readily detachable irrelevances were the castings out of demons, a projection of the crude demonology of the time, and the belief in His second Advent. This reduced Christology went hand in hand with the Ritschlian philosophy; in Theology there were no valid 'judgments of fact', but only 'judgments of value', so that there could no longer be any Christian dogma about Jesus, but only the value-judgment that He is the divinest of men, and in Him there are 'the values of God'.

(h) Likewise there was a denial of the miraculous, on account of the uniformity of nature and the universal validity of the laws of nature. Some of the Gospel miracles might be accepted, as faith-healings. But the Virgin-birth of our Lord was incredible in itself and irrelevant to His message and mission; and while we can believe that He survived death, as men in general do, and while there is no reason to doubt that His disciples saw visions of Him as risen, no resurrection of His body did in fact take place.

To the original 'Fundamentalists' it was a matter of vital importance that every one of the points which we have mentioned should be met with a direct denial; and as we have seen, they were supported by the testimony of some distinguished scholars.

The early years of this century were indeed a highly difficult time for the Christian apologist. Liberal Protestantism was at the height of its power; and about the same time 'Modernism' appeared also in the Roman Catholic Church. The Catholic Modernists, of whom the outstanding leaders were Alfred Loisy in France and George Tyrrell in England, accepted in general the points which we have listed, but gave them a Catholic turn; even if the miracles were not true, at least the Catholic religion grew out of the mission of Jesus and His apostles, and it was vastly preferable to the Protestantism of Harnack.

The Papal action against Modernism—the promulgation of the encyclical *Pascendi gregis* and of the syllabus of errors entitled *Lamentabili*, which condemned all the critical theories about the dates and origin of the biblical books, and the ex-communication of the chief Modernist leaders—took place in 1907, two years before the issue of 'The Fundamentals' began.

We may note also that the same period of unsettlement saw the spread of the sects which the producers of 'The Fundamentals' felt it necessary to denounce. Of these, at least the 'Jehovah's Witnesses' and the 'Seventh Day Adventists' are Fundamentalists in the strict sense, since they assume the complete infallibility and inerrancy of the text of the Bible, and add interpretations of their own which are imposed as of obligation on their adherents.

The position has, however, been completely altered since that time by the rise of the Biblical Theology, of which the great protagonist in England was Sir Edwyn Hoskyns. It can be said to date from the publication in 1931 of *The Riddle of the New Testament*, by Hoskyns and Davey, which remains to this day one of its most important books. Since then, the collapse of 'Liberal Theology' (in the sense in which we have been using the term) has been complete. The characteristic of this Biblical Theology is that it is at once deeply orthodox in faith, and thoroughly critical—more critical than the Liberal critics, since it is also critical of the critics themselves.

The key-point is that these scholars set themselves to seek to understand, in the first place, what it is that the biblical writers were intending to say to the men of their own time. They endeavour to see the Bible 'from within'; not to impose on it standards of judgment derived from any modern belief in 'progress', but to sit at their feet and learn from them what it was that they were seeking to express. Because no-one can do this unless he himself believes that what the biblical writers were expressing was in fact true, these Biblical Theologians are with few exceptions believing men. And because the endeavour is to determine what it was in fact that the writers were saying, this study is first of all a scientific study. Hence the opening words of *The Riddle of the New Testament* are (after a quotation of part of the Nicene Creed):

'When the Catholic Christian kneels at the words *incarnatus est* or at the words *and was incarnate*, he marks with proper solemnity his recognition that the Christian Religion has its origin neither in general religious experience, nor in some peculiar esoteric mysticism, nor in a dogma, and he declares his faith to rest on a particular event in history. Nor is the Catholic Christian peculiar in this concentration of faith. This is Christian Orthodoxy, both Catholic and Protestant. In consequence the Christian Religion is not merely open to historical investigation, but demands it, and its piety depends upon it. Inadequate or false reconstruction of the history of Jesus of Nazareth cuts at the heart of Christianity. The critical and historical study of the New Testament is therefore the prime activity of the Church. The recognition of the paramount importance of a particular history and of the necessity of a critical reconstruction of it is not new in the life of the Church. What is new is the emergence during the past two centuries of a precise method of handling historical evidence and an unshakeable confidence in the adequacy of the new method.'

And the final paragraph is: 'Here, then, the historian is driven to lay down his pen, not because he is defeated; not because his material has proved incapable of historical treatment; but because he is now forced by his own results to judge—to believe or to disbelieve. If the results of historical criticism be justified, the readers of the New Testament must make that judgment also.'

So the function of the critical scholar is related to his function as simple believer. The original 'Fundamentalists' were hindered from taking this line by the fact that—to put it in plain words—in their day much biblical criticism was heretical, and was also, as we see now, bad criticism.

The result of this endeavour of modern Biblical Theology to see the Bible 'from within' is that the Old Testament is now no longer disparaged. It is studied in the light of the faith which the writers themselves believed, the faith of Israel in the living God. It is seen as the Book of the People of God; and its prophets look forward from the incompleteness of the Old Covenant to its fulfilment in the New Covenant, in the coming 'Day of the Lord'. Since the New Testament books were all written in the faith that this fulfilment had taken place through the coming of Jesus of Nazareth and His death and resurrection, it is plain that the Bible forms one whole. The student of the New Testament is driven back at every point to the study of the words and the thought-forms of the Old Testament without which it is unintelligible. Thus the sense of the unity of the Bible has been recovered. In the next chapter we shall begin our study of the problem of biblical interpretation by an account of the contents of the Bible along these lines.

But we cannot conclude this chapter without paying tribute to the writers of those booklets on 'The Fundamentals'. They set out to proclaim the authority of the Lord God and of His Christ over the whole world and over every man. The word 'authority' is to be stressed. If the Gospel of God is not proclaimed with authority, it is not being proclaimed as the Word of God, but is being put forward as a human religious belief, which a man may adopt if he finds it reasonable. The Gospel of God demands therefore from us men that which the New Testament calls 'the obedience of faith'. The original 'Fundamentalists' knew this; and their successors too have known how to call out from men not a half-unwilling, half-persuaded assent, but the entire devotion of their hearts. Many who criticize Fundamentalism seem to be little aware of the missionary

24

work that has been done and is being done now, and of the whole surrender of lives to our Lord that lies behind it. Perhaps the word would be generally used now as a title of honour if we were all more alive to the Christian significance of its derivation.

The word 'fundamental' takes us back to the biblical word 'foundation'; it is a word that lies at the heart of the biblical message. The prophet Isaiah said in the Lord's name to the politicians at Jerusalem, during the 'war of nerves' when it seemed probable that the city might be destroyed any year in the near future, 'Behold, I lay in Zion for a foundation a stone, a tried stone, a precious corner-stone of sure foundation; he that believeth shall not make haste', or as Dr Dodd translates it, 'shall not hurry distractedly to and fro'.[1] And the psalmist of Ps. 118: 'The stone which the builders rejected is become the head of the corner; this is the Lord's doing; it is marvellous in our eyes' (vv. 22–3). The second of these texts is quoted by our Lord, in His reply to the chief priests after the cleansing of the temple, when He has just told the parable of the Wicked Husbandmen, and in it told of the rejection of the prophets and of His own coming death: He applies the words to Himself.[2] It is quoted again by St Peter to the Sanhedrin a few weeks later: 'He is the stone which was set at nought of you the builders, which was made the head of the corner. And in none other is there salvation; for neither is there any other Name under heaven, that is given among men, wherein we must be saved.'[3] That the one Foundation is Christ is said by St Paul in I Cor. 3.11; on Him as the head corner-stone the Church of God is built.[4] In I Peter 2.5 the Lord is a living stone, on whom the Christians as living stones are built up as a spiritual temple; in the verses that follow, Isa. 28.16 and Ps. 118.22 are both quoted, and the same Stone is said to be 'a stone of stumbling and a rock of offence',[5] on which those who do not believe stumble and fall. Rom. 9.33 conflates the texts, and applies them to unbelieving Israel.

Our Lord came making an absolute claim of authority. In

[1] Isa. 28. 16. Dodd, *The Interpretation of the Fourth Gospel*, p. 179.
[2] Mark 12. 10–11.   [3] Acts 4. 11–12.
[4] Eph. 2. 20–2.   [5] Isa. 8. 14.

the gospels, 'to have eternal life', 'to enter into the Kingdom of God' and to 'follow Me' are synonyms,[1] and to 'follow Me' is to deny the self (not, to deny things to the self); it is to lose the self, to surrender the self, as the only way in which the self can be found again.[2] So St Paul calls Baptism a death to the old self, 'being buried with Christ in his death', and being raised up in him to share by faith and hope His risen life, through the Spirit.[3]

This note of the authority of the Gospel of God is heard throughout church history, when the Word of God is proclaimed to the Jews who have rejected Him, or to a church which has become lax and worldly. Martyrs give their lives, the early monks go out into the desert, St Athanasius suffers for the Faith, St Augustine witnesses to the grace of God against the Pelagian claim to salvation by good works, St Francis embraces a life of poverty, the Reformers reassert the Gospel of the grace of God, St Ignatius Loyola leaves all to become a soldier of Christ—a great cloud of witnesses: and in our day too there are heroic figures such as C. T. Studd, Hudson Taylor, Mary Slessor, Amy Carmichael.

The note of the Divine Imperative is still heard, not least among those whom the world calls Fundamentalists, in the missionary call to heathen lands overseas and the missionary work in the home-lands; it is heard in the midst of a church life that has become easy and comfortable, accommodated to the standards of the world; young people hear it, who have been brought up with a Christian education in which they have learnt to repeat holy phrases, but have never learnt for themselves what they mean; middle-aged people hear it, who have lived the best part of their lives without any real faith in God, and out of an aimless life in which they find no rest for their souls come with the joy of discovery to find joy and peace in the surrender of their lives to God.

For our civilization is in confusion. We are busy over many things, making money, devising new and wonderful gadgets for flight over land and ocean, restless in seeking to save our

---

[1] Mark 10. 17, 21, 23, etc.   [2] Mark 8. 34–5   [3] Rom. 6. 3–6.

civilization from what we call the Communist peril; but not getting down to the real truth of things and the knowledge of ourselves, not reflecting that the true defence against Communism would be to find out, somehow, how to approach the Communists as fellow-men and brothers and discover the way to a real interchange of thought with them. Our civilization has lost its centre, because it has lost the way to God and put Man in the centre instead.

And here is I.V.F., with its splendid witness to the authority of the Gospel of God over men's personal lives and the saving of their individual souls. Here it stands in the line of the biblical and Christian tradition. But what has it to say about God's world, and the problems of our social life? For it is not sufficient to say that if only individuals are converted and give their hearts to God all will be well; it is still necessary for them to know how they are to live their lives after they are converted, amid all the problems of business, commerce and social relations.

And here is S.C.M., bravely setting out to tackle the whole problem of Christian living, those of social life, and of Biblical criticism, and of the unity of all Christians, and all the rest; and these problems are so pressing and so complicated that, however much one tries to find the Christian way, one is in danger of becoming immersed in the discussion of problems and yet more problems, and losing sight of the one thing needful—the knowledge of God Himself.

S.C.M. and I.V.F. find it difficult to work together; they pursue separate paths, not helping one another. The one is seeking the salvation of the whole man, and of the social life in which he is immersed; the other, the entire conversion of the individual to God. Can they not come together, for the sake of what each has to give to the other, to God's glory?

III

The Bible and God's Saving Purpose

THE Bible starts with Adam and not with Abraham. It would assuredly have started with Abraham, if its chief concern were to relate the remarkable religious development of a specially gifted nation. But actually it presupposes the faith of that nation in the Lord, the God who made the worlds. Therefore it must start with the creation by God of the whole universe. Then it must speak of Adam, of Man as God created him, and as he actually is; created to live in dependence upon God, receiving from Him the gift of life and all the good things of the world, and thanking Him for everything; but now disobedient to God, a rebel, grabbing greedily at God's gifts, and putting the Self in place of God. Thus we have the story of Adam and Eve; and this, with the following stories of the Flood and the Tower of Babel, forms the *Preface* to the Bible. The problem has been posed: God created man good, but man has become corrupt. What then did God do?

God called Abraham. This begins the *Introduction* to the main story, which covers the rest of the Book of Genesis. In a magnificent sentence in Gal. 3.8 St Paul sets out a whole philosophy of history, discerning a continuity in the Purpose of God from the call of Abraham, that in him all nations might be blessed, to the final term of that Purpose in the justification of the Gentiles by faith. The principle of it is what he calls in Rom. 9.11 the 'Purpose according to Selection'; first a family is chosen, then a nation, till at last all nations can be called to share in the blessing of God's Salvation. So Abraham is chosen (and not Lot), Isaac (and not Ishmael), Jacob (and not Esau); and Jacob is the ancestor of the twelve tribes of Israel.

Now the *Main Story* begins, with the Exodus. The people whom God has chosen are in bondage in Egypt; not yet a nation. In the Exodus God delivers them with a mighty hand and an outstretched arm, makes His Covenant with them at Horeb, thereby uniting them to Himself as His chosen nation; gives to them through Moses His Law (but the word *Torah* means much more than 'rules'; it means the knowledge of God's will and His ways); and brings them, with His presence among them symbolized by the Ark of the Covenant, into the land of Canaan.

The rest of the Main Story is best summarized by a series of three statements of the Faith of Israel, at three stages in the history:

(A) *The Faith of Israel in the pre-exilic period*, say in the middle period of the monarchy: 'We believe in the Lord (Yahweh, Jehovah) our God, who delivered us out of Egypt, made His Covenant with us, led us into the Promised Land, and dwells in our midst in "the place which he has chosen to set his name there"; and we hope in Him that He will accomplish His good Purpose for us.'

But Israel, as the prophets taught, was a backsliding and sinful nation, and it fell under the Lord's judgment. Samaria was destroyed in 721 B.C., Jerusalem fell in 586 B.C., and the survivors were deported to Mesopotamia.

(B) *The Faith of Israel in exile*, when the surviving remnant had learnt the lesson which the prophets taught: 'We believe in the Lord our God (as in A above). But we sinned fearfully against Him, and He chastized us by the ruin of our existence as a nation and the destruction of the Temple, the City and our homes. Yet the very fact of His chastizement of us means that He has a future in store for us; and taught by His prophets we hope for a Second Exodus-deliverance, from the lands of our exile;[1] a new Covenant, by which His *Torah* shall be written in our hearts, and we shall truly know Him;[2] the outpouring of His Spirit upon us, the Spirit which spake by the prophets, that we may obey His will;[3] the return of His presence to dwell in

[1] Jer. 23. 7–8, etc.   [2] Jer. 31. 31–4.   [3] Ezek. 36. 27.

29

our midst in a restored sanctuary;[1] and finally the coming in of all nations to share in this knowledge of Him which we have been privileged to have.'[2]

There was a return of many of the exiles to Jerusalem, and the Temple was rebuilt; but still the promised Day of the Lord's deliverance had not come. Synagogues were built, in which the People of God met to praise God and to pray to Him and to hear His Law read and expounded. There was a fierce attack on Israel's faith and worship in the second century B.C., in which there were thousands of martyrs, and also a successful holy war, through which the temple worship was restored. But still the promised Day did not come.

(C) *The Faith of the Apostolic Church:* 'We believe in the Lord God of Israel (as in A and B above). But now the promised Day has come, in the person of Jesus the Messiah, the Son of God, and in Him all is fulfilled: the Second Exodus, in His death and resurrection;[3] the New Covenant, ratified by Him in a sacramental rite in the night on which He was betrayed;[4] the outpouring of the Spirit at Pentecost[5] and continually since, to make possible the new life 'in Christ'; the divine presence restored, in the Word who was made flesh and tabernacled among us, so that we beheld His glory[6]—yet not a presence in the temple at Jerusalem made with hands, but in the true Temple which is His body and is built of living stones[7]—and finally, the Gospel proclaimed to all nations, and multitudes of Gentiles admitted to share in the inheritance of old Israel, as the New Israel, the People of God.[8] All is fulfilled, and yet not completely fulfilled; for we look forward to the Last Advent of our Lord and the final establishment of His eternal and glorious Kingdom, when all the sin of man shall have been done away and God's Purpose for man shall be complete.'

The Bible tells the story of a mighty drama, in which God is the chief actor and man is seen as the object of His mercy, learning from generation to generation, through much suffering,

[1] Ezek. 43. 1–7.　　[2] Isa. 45. 22–3; Ps. 86. 9–10.　[3] I Cor. 5. 7–8.
[4] I Cor. 11. 25.　　[5] Acts 2.　　　　　　　　[6] John 1. 14.
[7] I Peter 2. 4–5.　　[8] Gal. 3. 28–9.

the lessons which God wills to teach him. It is the history of God's saving action, as seen by man whom God is seeking and saving: much as the Parable of the Lost Sheep might be imagined as being told not by an outside observer but by the sheep which is rescued.

Let us now consider some points which arise out of this summary of the contents of the Bible.

(i) *What is the meaning of the word 'canonical'*, as applied to Scripture? In other words, in what relation do the books of the Bible stand in relation to the tradition of the Faith of Israel, which was handed down from father to son through the whole period of the history?

In the case of the New Testament, the facts are plain enough. The books were canonized in order to preserve the tradition of the apostles' teaching about the events of the Redemption, and their meaning, and the way of life which the Christians must follow. 'Tradition' is a biblical word; St Paul speaks of two traditions of first-rate importance which he had 'received' and had 'delivered' to them, about the Last Supper and about the Resurrection[1], and of traditions of ethical behaviour.[2] The Pauline epistles are believed to have been formed into a collection somewhere about A.D. 100; the New Testament as a whole took shape about A.D. 170, substantially as it is now, in order to preserve the authentic apostolic tradition, in place of the garbled version of these books put out by Marcion the heretic, and to exclude the Docetist writings in which our Lord's true humanity was denied.

Similarly with regard to the Old Testament: the function of the books was to guard the tradition and form a canon or standard of what was to be believed about God, about the facts of the history, and about the way of life of the People of God; here the record of the events of the Exodus and the Covenant was of primary importance, as giving the foundation of Israel's own existence as the Chosen People. At the time of the Exile, when so many traditions had been broken it was specially im-

[1] I Cor. 11. 23 ff.; 15. 1 ff.   [2] II Thess. 3. 6 ff.

portant to preserve the history of the preceding period; the Books of Kings, which were edited during the Exile, lay stress on the sins for which Israel had suffered the Lord's judgment; and the books of the prophets were preserved because they had announced His judgment. Thus the books of the Bible set the *canon* or standard of the faith and the way of life of the People of God; and so they do to-day, for the Church.

(ii) *The Word and the Spirit.* A theory has been held in recent years that the Revelation consists essentially in the acts of God Himself, in the deliverance of Israel from Egypt, His judgment on her in the exile, the coming of the Son of God in the Incarnation; and that the books of the Bible contain the human record of these things, as described and interpreted by faithful but fallible men. In this view the Bible, consisting of 'words of men', is no more than a human record of and commentary on God's mighty acts of salvation.

This is indeed to stress as 'the fundamentals' the mighty acts of God. But what has happened to the doctrine of the Holy Spirit? The implication is that, in the events recorded in the New Testament, God sent His Son and in Him revealed His glory, and then left us men to trace out according to our poor human notions the works of His mighty wisdom, and (presumably also) to follow as best we could so great an Example. But this rigid separation between the Word of God and the words of men simply will not do. It is to make a separation between the Son of God and the Spirit; and it is contradicted, in both Testaments, by the biblical narrative itself.

God redeems Israel out of Egypt; but at the same time He sends Moses to interpret by the Spirit what He is doing. Moses is spoken of in the Old Testament as the greatest of the prophets: 'There hath not arisen a prophet since in Israel like unto Moses, whom the Lord knew face to face.'[1] Again, the word which the Holy Ghost spake by the prophets from Amos and Hosea onwards is grouped round the period of God's judgment on Israel in the exile: before it, during it, after it. When this great period of crisis is over, prophecy begins to die down. Again, when God

[1] Deut. 4.310, the concluding sentence of the Pentateuch.

sent His Son, He sent also the Holy Spirit, the Paraclete, whose supreme function was and is to show to us Christ: 'He shall bear witness of me', 'He shall take of mine and shall show it unto you'.[1] 'And ye also shall bear witness'; having received the Spirit, the apostles are sent as witnesses of the Resurrection, of the fact and of its meaning. So it is at the central points in the Bible history; and throughout the Bible the Holy Spirit is working in men, speaking His divine Word through their human words, guiding, teaching, giving life.

(iii) *Some parts of the Bible stand nearer to the centre than others.* This is so plain that it scarcely needs to be illustrated. The stories of the Creation and the Fall, Abraham, Moses and the Exodus, David, Isaiah's prophecies and those of his great successors, the gospels and the great epistles—it is here that most of the lessons come which are read oftenest in the church service, and the place to which the Bible reader most often turns. He goes to Isaiah 40 or 53 or Jeremiah 31, or to St John or to Romans, rather than to Ecclesiastes or Esther, to II Peter or Jude.

But when we have said this, we must at once add that the whole Bible is canonical, and that there is a connection between canonicity and inspiration. There are indeed the 'central' parts of Scripture which mark the key-points of the working out of God's Purpose, as distinguished from those which are mere episodes. But every book which was admitted to the Canon was admitted because it had something to give, because some Word of God was spoken in it. So, for instance, Ecclesiastes makes a needed protest against the too docile orthodoxy which indulges in wishful thinking, and expresses a scepticism which sees the vanity of all things apart from faith in God; and Esther tells the story of a brave woman trusting in God and His providence over Israel at the risk of her life, and we get the great sentence, 'Who knoweth whether thou art not come to the kingdom for such a time as this?'[2]

It was the Church, the Jewish Church in the one case and the Christian in the other, which decided which books must be accepted and which excluded. From this it is sometimes

[1] John 15.26; 16.14.   [2] Esth. 4.14.

wrongly inferred that the Church conferred authority on the books of the Bible by her choice of them; the Church, having God's revelation, proceeded to select those books which were according to her mind; and thus the Church, having been in existence before the books were written, has a certain lordship over the Bible. This is to get the matter gravely wrong. The Church did exist before the Bible, and the books were written within the Church, and later formed into a Canon of Scripture by the Church; but the Church is subject to the Lord, and depends on Him for her salvation. So, living by the tradition of faith, that is, of faith in Him, and indwelt by the Spirit, she has known and knows now what are the books that testify of Him. The Vatican Council got *this* point right when it said that 'the Church regards them as sacred and canonical, not because having been framed solely by human labour they have afterwards been approved by her authority, not again for the reason that they contain the revelation without error, but because having been written by the inspiration of the Holy Spirit they have God as their author, and *as such have been given to the Church*'.[1] And so also Archdeacon T. C. Hammond points out the need of distinguishing between 'recognition of authority and authority itself. The Church recognized the Sacred Scriptures as being God's message to man, and published abroad its conviction. But that conviction could only find a sound base in the inherent power of the Scriptures themselves.'[2]

(iv) That *Prophecy is recognized in the Bible as prediction* is seen clearly in our summary outline. Our Lord and His apostles endorse the anticipations of the coming Day of the Lord which the prophets had given; it is said repeatedly that the prophecies are fulfilled. Yet during the Liberal period it was continually being said that the prophets were forth-tellers rather than fore-tellers, and that the real importance of the prophecies was that they proclaimed a right belief about God, and applied that belief to the circumstances of their time in their moral teaching and their condemnation of social iniquity. But in fact we find

---

[1] Denzinger, *Enchiridion Symbolorum*, § 1787. Italics mine. Cf. p. 56 below.
[2] T. C. Hammond, *Inspiration and Authority*, I.V.F., p. 56, cf. p. 60 below.

in the Old Testament two criteria by which the 'true prophet' is to be distinguished from the false prophet; the first is, whether he speaks in the Name of the Lord God and not of other gods,[1] and similarly in Jer. 23.15–40, whether he has 'stood in the Lord's council' to 'perceive and hear His word' (v. 18), and does not give the people instead some dream that he has dreamed (vv. 25 ff.) or other notions of his own heart. The second is, whether the thing foretold comes to pass.[2]

Yet the prophets are not mere predicters, like the astrologers of that day and of this; that which they predict is the future course of God's saving action. They endeavour to discern the shape of the coming Deliverance. Such is the interpretation of prophecy in I Peter 1.10–11, where they are pictured as straining their eyes to discern what person or what time[3] the Spirit of the Messiah which was in them was pointing to, when He testified beforehand of the sufferings of the Messiah and the glory that should follow. It is implied here that the fulfilment which came in Christ was greater and deeper than the prophet was able to grasp; and the same is implied in Hebrews 1.1–2, where it is said that God who of old spoke in the prophets *polymerōs kai polytropōs*, in many partial ways and many different styles, has in the end of those days spoken to us in His Son, once for all and inclusively. So for instance Isaiah predicted the coming of a King of David's line who in the Day of the Lord should sit on the throne of David and rule in righteousness.[4] There came a King of David's line; but when He came, He steadily refused the idea of a Messiah wielding political power. He is indeed King, but King in a wider and deeper sense, proclaiming and exercising a rule over men's hearts and consciences, a King who came bearing witness to the truth, the universal spiritual King who has entered on His Kingdom not by worldly success but by being lifted up on a cross and from there drawing all men unto Him.[5]

It is this theological fulfilment that is emphasized throughout the New Testament; indeed it is a main preoccupation of the

[1] Deut. 18. 20.   [2] Deut. 18. 21–2; Jer. 28. 9, cf. vv. 15–17.
[3] So the *Revised Standard Version* translates I Peter 1. 11, and surely it is right.
[4] Isa. 11. 1–9.   [5] John 12. 32; 18. 36–7.

35

New Testament writers to show how the Old Testament prophecies have been fulfilled in this way: with regard to the fulfilment of the Law,[1] the meaning of the Lord's passion, the fulfilment of sacrifice, the promise of the outpouring of the Spirit, the preaching of the Gospel to all nations, and a variety of other things. It is here that the stress lies, and not on the interesting small fulfilments of details, such as Bethlehem as the place of the Nativity, or the fact that at the crucifixion the soldiers cast lots for His vesture.[2] This is a point which Christian interpreters have often failed, and fail, to notice.

In the light of this, we can well ask ourselves what is the true line of interpretation of the Book of the Revelation, which is the one great book of Christian prophecy that we have. What was the message which St John himself wished that we his readers should look for in his book? Was it that we should decipher correctly the meaning of the '666' in Rev. 13.18? or 17.8–11, where it seems that the next but one after the reigning emperor is to be the embodiment of Antichrist? or the Millennium in 20.4–6? Or was it rather that we should meditate upon and take to heart the visions of the glory of God and the heavenly worship in chapters 4 and 5, and of the risen Christ in chapter 1 —the glory of the Church's faith and hope, set forth in the canticles of praise—the warnings of the letting loose of all the powers of evil in the coming apostasy and the manifestation of Antichrist—the Christian conflict, and the victory beyond all conflict to be won by faithfulness unto death—the certainty of the Lord's Advent and His glorious Kingdom? All this, and above all that we should fear lest we should be unfaithful and fall away. 'He that hath an ear, let him hear what the Spirit saith unto the Churches.' St. John certainly believed that he was an inspired prophet; he tells us so. In what did *he* believe that his inspiration lay? What did he think was the message which God had committed to him?

(v) The *Fall of Man* stands out in our outline summary as the evident presupposition of the history which the Bible relates of God's Purpose for man's salvation. It tells us that in the begin-

[1] Rom. 13. 8–10.   [2] Mark 15. 24; John. 19.24.

ning God saw all that He had made, and behold it was very good. But man as we see him is not so; and throughout the Bible man is seen as sinful and in need of salvation. To quote the late Dr Griffith Thomas:[1]

'If it be said that the doctrine of the Fall, found in Genesis and again in the teaching of St Paul, is not found elsewhere in the Old Testament, the answer is that "the whole tenor of the Scriptural representation of man" points in the direction of sinfulness as due to its entrance at the beginning of the race, for "at no point in Scripture history does man appear as standing in right or normal relation with God." So that the only conclusion that seems reasonable is that "if a Fall were not narrated in the opening chapters of Genesis we should still have to postulate something of the kind to account for the Bible's own representation of the state of man".'

This is very interesting; for it suggests that belief in the actuality of the Fall is so much one of the fundamentals of our faith that it is more fundamental than belief that the account in Genesis is literally true as a factual record. God made man in His own image, as the Scripture says; a few pages later it says, 'And God saw the earth, and behold it was corrupt, for all flesh had corrupted his (its) way upon the earth,'[2] and such is man to-day. It follows that man has failed to be what God intended him to be, and that can only have been by his own choice; somehow, at some point, man took a wrong turning. This is what is asserted in Genesis 3; that man succumbed to temptation from outside himself, and fell away into rebellion against God, choosing to be as God, and setting up the Self as his object of worship in place of God. If on the other hand there was no Fall, or if the Fall was really 'a fall upwards', or if the sin of man has not been due to temptation from outside but to some innate perversity in man's own nature, it follows that man was not created good. In this case the Redemption will not be a 'buying back' (redemption) of man to become

---

[1] W. Griffith Thomas, *The Principles of Theology: an Introduction to the Thirty-nine Articles*, London 1930, p. 164. The quotations which he makes are from James Orr, *God's Image in Man*, pp. 198 and 201.

[2] Gen. 6.12.

what God intended him to be, a restoration in man of the divine image and likeness, but will be a stage in man's evolution from lower to higher—in other words, not a redemption at all.

Such is the theological issue which underlies Genesis 2 and 3. But when we turn to examine these chapters as historians, we have to ask the usual questions: From what witnesses can the narrative have been derived? How was the story handed down till it came to be written down? and there is no satisfying answer. If there was a tradition of the Fall handed down from the very beginnings of our race, we should expect to find traces of it among many nations; and this does not appear to be the case. There was indeed a Paradise-myth known to Ezekiel, as appears from Ezek. 28.12–19; but Genesis 2 and 3 would be known to him. In Babylonian and Accadian myths there are some slight resemblances to the Genesis story;[1] but nothing approaching a tradition of a Fall. The purely historical evidence for the literal and factual truth of the narrative appears to be nil.

What then are we to say, as historians and as theologians? There are four possibilities:

(a) To cling to the factual character of the story, in spite of historical-critical difficulties. We affirm that there was a Fall. Scripture contains a story of a Fall. Therefore the story is to be taken as literally true. A serpent did actually stand on its tail and speak with a human voice.

(b) To say, with the Liberals generally, that the story in Genesis is simply a 'myth'; the meaning is that it is simply untrue. This is expressed as follows in a recent book:

'The stories of the Creation and the Fall are also legends explaining the origin of customs and institutions; that is to say, they are aetiological legends. In these two dramatic stories the Hebrews found answers to many questions dealing with human life and interests. When were clothes first worn? Why are serpents hated by man? Why do they crawl along the ground? Why is man mortal? And in particular, questions relating to

[1] See S. H. Hooke, *In the Beginning* (The Clarendon Bible; Old Testament, Vol. VI), 1947, pp. 28–30.

sex: What causes sexual attraction? When was marriage insti-
tuted? Why is woman subservient to man? Why is birth
painful?'[1]

Simply from the point of view of literary criticism, this account
is most reprehensible. The writer has no appreciation of the
profound theological truth of the story and the insight of the
writer. One of our greatest contemporary theologians, Rein-
hold Niebuhr, says, 'the profundity of the account of the Fall
cannot be over-estimated'. On the theological side, Liberal
Theology has consistently rejected the doctrine of the Fall. The
Fall was a fall upwards; the evil in man is immaturity and imperfection, which (we hope) he is in process of outgrowing. That
is not an easy thesis for us of the middle twentieth century to
accept; we have seen Mussolini, Hitler and Stalin. There is no
real explanation here of the facts of human life as we know them.

(c) To say, with many good Christians to-day, that the story
of Adam and Eve is a true and inspired 'parable' of man's actual
condition. The word *'adam* means 'man'; Eve is the Hebrew
hivvah, 'life'; she is the mother. Adam and Eve stand for Mr
and Mrs Jones, and the story depicts most truly the root of evil
which is in us all, as is shown in our temptations and our sins
day by day. But it is not merely that the story is not literally
and factually true; it is not true at all, as history. There was not,
at the beginning of our race, such a catastrophe as it depicts.

So Professor Alan Richardson writes:

'The time-element in the myths of Creation and Fall (as in
all the biblical myths) must be discounted: it is not that *once*
(in 4004 B.C.—or a hundred thousand years ago) God created
man perfect and then he fell from grace. God is eternally
Creator; he is eternally making man and holding him in being
and seeing that his handiwork is good (Gen. 1.31). And just as
creation is an eternal activity, so the "Fall" is an ingredient of
every moment of human life; man is at every moment "falling",
putting himself in the centre, rebelling against the will of God.
Adam is Everyman.'[2]

[1] E. B. Redlich, *The Early Traditions of Genesis*, Duckworth, 1950, p. 74–5.
[2] Alan Richardson in the *Theological Word-book* (S.C.M.), edited by him, s.v.
'Adam', p. 14. Cf. his book, *Genesis I–XI* in the 'Torch' series, S.C.M., 1953.

I do not know what this means. I think it is mere playing with words to define the Creation and the Fall as that God is every moment creating and man every moment falling. I want to say that God created us good, and that there was a catastrophe far back in the past. I want to say that evil is not part of my nature. I fear that Professor Richardson is not allowing me to say this, any more than the old Liberals.

(iv) It remains to say that the story of Adam and Eve is not a factual historical narrative, but that it describes the historical truth, and that the writer intended it so; he wrote it as a ficti-tious Tale, to set forth the truth of that which he believed to have happened. I wish to call it a Tale, rather than a Myth. I think he wrote it, using material derived from folk-lore; per-haps the story of the making of Eve out of Adam's rib comes from some such source. But whatever his sources, he put into them a profound theological insight, derived from his know-ledge of God.

As was said in the first chapter, it is impossible in a book such as this to give anything more than brief and summary dis-cussions of great problems; and here is an instance of a subject which demands a whole treatise, covering the meanings of the word 'myth'; the doctrine of creation; speculations about a Fall of rebel angels; theories of the transmission of Original Sin; the relation between Sin and Death, and whether St Paul be-lieved that physical death was the result of sin, in view *both* of Rom. 5.12–14 and 8.6. I am neither discussing nor answering any of these questions here. I am only asserting that God made man, with the rest of His creation, 'very good', and that man has made of himself something very evil; and that this appears to involve a moral catastrophe somewhere in the pre-history of our race. But there is one further point to be made.

In one of the I.V.F. books[1] there is a wise remark: 'Chapters ii and iii (of Genesis) have much in common with the two closing chapters of Revelation, and in both it is hard to say where the literal ends and the symbolic begins.' Both the Beginning and the End of our universe are real; but both can be described by

[1] *The New Bible Handbook*, ed. G. T. Manley, I.V.F., 1947, p. 127.

us only in symbolic language. Of the Beginning itself, the creation, there were no human witnesses; of the Fall there were human participants, unable as yet to record their experience. Of the End there will be vast multitudes of human witnesses; but the Events that will happen then are beyond our present power to comprehend. At this point St Paul is forced to write, 'Behold, I show you a mystery: we shall not all sleep, but we shall all be changed'[1]—but changed into what? Into a resurrection-body that will be somehow continuous with this body, but will be transformed into something suited to conditions of existence which are utterly beyond our present experience.

[1] I Cor. 15. 51.

IV

The Truth of the Bible

THE study of the Word of God in the Bible needs to begin with the study of the Purpose of God for man's salvation which it proclaims, and which is fulfilled and consummated in Christ who is personally the Word of God. The study of the words of men through which this Word of God is made known to us must start with the particular word which each writer was endeavouring to say, in relation to the message of the Bible as a whole.

It is in this larger context that we need to study the words Inerrancy and Infallibility, which will occupy us for this and the next three chapters. They are troublesome and unsatisfactory words, *because they are negative words*, like the word 'sinless' applied to our Lord. He is indeed spoken of as sinless in John 8.46, in II Cor. 5.21, in Hebrews 4.15, in I Peter 2.22, and in each case the phrase has a special relevance to the context. But really we need positives such as 'We beheld His glory, glory as of the Only-begotten from the Father, full of grace and truth'[1]; or 'I do always the things that please him',[2] or 'the light of the knowledge of the glory of God in the face of Jesus Christ'.[3] So, we need positives to describe the inspiration of Scripture, as in the only two passages which speak of it directly: 'All Scripture is given by inspiration of God and is profitable. . . .' (A.V.), or 'Every Scripture inspired of God is profitable. . . .'[4] (R.V.), and 'No prophecy ever came by the will of man, but men spake from God, being moved by the Holy Ghost'.[5] These are positive phrases, speaking of 'inspiration' and 'the Holy Ghost'. The positives of Inerrancy and Infallibility might be 'true and faithful witness to the Truth of God'.

[1] John 1. 14. [2] John 8. 29. [3] II Cor. 4. 6.
[4] II Tim. 3. 16. [5] II Peter 1. 21.

In what senses then is it obligatory on all Christians to say that 'the Bible is true'?

First, *the Bible is true as history*, if it truly relates the working out in history of God's Purpose of salvation. We are justified here in distinguishing the main outline of the history and its cardinal events from episodes such as would never be mentioned in any summary of the history; such episodes as the history of Absalom's rebellion, or of the conversion of the Ethiopian eunuch in Acts 8. These are authentic historical narratives, but such that if they were legendary, or if the events had not been recorded, the main course of the history would scarcely be affected. But if the Exodus story were not in substance true, the faith of Israel about its own vocation would be grounded on a falsehood; and the same is true of our Lord's resurrection, as St Paul says in so many words: 'If Christ hath not been raised, your faith is vain; ye are yet in your sins'.[1] The truth of the Bible narrative of the working out of God's Purpose can be checked at all the main points by internal evidence—the marks of authenticity in the narratives themselves—and by external evidence, such as Assyrian inscriptions which tell us that Ahab fought in the Battle of Karkar, and enable us to fix many other dates in the history of that period, or the inscription which tells us that Gallio became proconsul of Achaia in A.D. 51. St Luke makes a careful reference to external history in his elaborate dating of the beginning of our Lord's ministry in Luke 3.1–2; the Creed does the same in the words 'suffered under Pontius Pilate'. We may reflect that it would raise difficulties for us if it could be proved that Pontius Pilate never existed.

But a rigid theory of the factual inerrancy of the Bible must be too narrow, as it seems, to allow for a satisfactory account of the story of Adam and Eve. We have seen that this story has symbolic elements in it, and it seems that it was written by its author as a fictitious Tale describing an actual event, and not as a factual description of that event exactly as it happened. As was said at the start of this chapter, we need to attend to that

[1] I Cor. 15. 17.

43

which each writer was intending to say; in other words, we must attend to the *genre* of each biblical writing. We must not interpret poetry as if it were prose, nor parables as records of events; we are not called upon to suppose that the speeches in the Book of Job are exact accounts of speeches actually made by Job and his friends, if the writer did not so intend them. If the author of the Book of Jonah was not intending to relate the actual history of Jonah the son of Amittai,[1] but rather a fictitious Tale intending to show the wrongness of the attitude of aloofness towards the Gentiles which many Jews were taking in the period after Ezra, we must interpret the book accordingly. The question is, Was that his intention?

When our Lord says 'A certain man was going down from Jerusalem to Jericho',[2] we are not required to hold that the Parable of the Good Samaritan is a literal record of fact; for the *genre* of the parable-story, when it is not an allegory, is that it expresses real truth by means of fiction, somewhat in the manner of a political cartoon. We have an excellent instance of a parable and its application in the Parable of the Two Sons.[3]

Or again, the gospels themselves have a *genre* which is all their own. They are not in the least like the modern style of biography; we are told only one story about His boyhood, nothing about His early manhood; there is no description of His character, no critical appreciation of His life-work. The gospels are all proclamations of The Gospel, as it is set forth in the events of the coming into the world of the Saviour of the world, of His ministry, of His death and His resurrection. That which St John writes of his gospel is true equally of the others: 'Many other signs therefore did Jesus in the presence of his disciples which are not written in this book; but these are written, that ye may believe that Jesus is the Christ, the Son of God, and that believing ye may have life in his name.'[4] St. John's gospel too must be interpreted according to what the evangelist intended it to be. If he was intending to write a

---

[1] II Kings 14. 25.   [2] Luke 10. 30.
[3] Matt. 21. 28–32.   [4] John 20. 30–1.

theological history, primarily in order to show the real inwardness of the mission and work of the Son of God incarnate, it could be that he was allowing himself certain liberties with regard to the mere literal facts. He does indeed lay the greatest stress on the factual character of the story of Jesus, as real history;[1] but we may well be missing much of what he really intends us to learn from his book if we spend our time of study largely in proving the literal and factual character of every detail. Here and in all the books of the Bible we must attend to what the writer is intending to say. We must take the books as they are, and not impose on them our own notion of what they ought to be.

Second, *the Bible is true as conveying to us the revelation of the living and true God*. We see now that the old Liberals were seriously wrong in interpreting the revelation of God in too intellectual a way, and supposing that in the development of religion there came a point where the prophetic writers passed from monolatry, the demand that one God only is to be worshipped, to monotheism, the belief that one God only exists. This was to treat the Hebrews as if they were Greeks. The prophets did indeed believe that there is one God only. But the emphasis was rather on the *reality* of God, that God must be taken seriously, that He is to be feared; that He was not a personification of the genius of the nation, like the Britannia on a British penny, that He was not a god made in man's image, but that man was made in His. It is for this reason that the Old Testament has such a horror of graven and molten images. Let me give a pair of illustrations of this.

David was 'a man after the Lord's own heart', a devoted servant of the Lord, but also capable of great cruelty to the enemies of his nation, and guilty of great sins. But the point is this: Did he treat the religious devotion of his people as a valuable political asset to him as king—we can think of kings and ecclesiastics in many centuries who have performed religious rituals for the sake of the impression that they made on

[1] Cf. John 19. 35.

the people, irrespective of any belief of their own that they were true—or did he really fear God? David committed a great sin when he fell in love with Bathsheba and made arrangements for her husband to fall in battle. An Ahab and a Jezebel would think nothing of this, as their treatment of Naboth shows; not so David. Nathan came to him and showed him what he had done; and David confessed, 'I have sinned against the Lord.'[1]

Three centuries later the prophets are convicting Israel of sin, and threatening God's judgment. With Sennacherib's army in the country, the Assyrian Rabshakeh points out to the people on the wall how the tribal gods of Hamath and Arpad, Sepharvaim and Henna and Ivvah have all in turn been overwhelmed, and argues that the God of Israel, who has not been able to save Samaria, will try in vain to save Jerusalem.[2] This states the question which became actual for the people of Jerusalem when Jerusalem did fall in 586 B.C.: would they assent to this, and in the land of exile become merged in the Mesopotamian proletariate? The faithful remnant, helped by Jeremiah and Ezekiel, made their act of heroic faith and repentance: 'The prophets were right. The Lord God is faithful and true, and He is in control. We have sinned and He has justly chastized us by the ruin of our city and nation.' So Israel passed through a death to a resurrection of life.

But it is in our Lord that the revelation of God is fulfilled and completed. We must now see how this comes to pass. We shall see that the doctrine of the Inerrancy of Scripture in all its parts is again too narrow to cover the facts, because the Old Testament, taken by itself, is incomplete and even erroneous till it comes to be fulfilled in Him. And this time the error is not in small matters of literal fact, but in matters of faith and morals.

All Christians acknowledge that the Law is incomplete and imperfect as compared with the Gospel. Our Lord says in the Sermon on the Mount, 'Ye have heard how it was said to them of old time . . . but I say unto you . . .'[3] The Old Testament was God's Word, but it was not His final Word. In times past, and

[1] II Sam. 12.13.   [2] II Kings 18.33-5.   [3] Matt. 5.21-2, 27-8, 33-4, 38-9, 43-4.

to-day, Christians have often been misled through not attending to this fact, and so thinking, for instance, that they had scriptural warrant for going out to fight their enemies in the spirit of Saul or David fighting Amalek, or, as in South Africa to-day, treating the African races as Canaanites, meant to be hewers of wood and drawers of water. This was and is a misuse of the Bible, through failure to see the Bible as a whole.

We will take three points, all of them important: first, the tendency to legalism in the Old Testament; second, its tendency to a wrong nationalism; and third, the invocations of vengeance on enemies in the psalms.

(i) *The tendency to legalism.* Israel had God's Law. Therefore she was tempted to legalism, substituting the keeping of commandments for the real service of God.

It comes first in this way. The prophets pronounce the judgment of God on the people's sins: sins such as idolatry, in forsaking the Lord and going after the nature-religions of Canaan, or a false worship of Him without faith and repentance, or 'grinding the faces of the poor'. If they go on sinning, they will suffer for it. But if they turn again and repent, will not God spare them? So the matter is stated often, as for instance in Deut. 28, where in verses 1–14 they have the promise of God's blessing if they are faithful and keep His commandments, and in verses 15–68 the curse which will follow them if they disobey.

Ezekiel is very explicit about this. 'The soul that sinneth, it shall die; the son shall not bear the iniquity of the father.'[1] The Israelites in exile were saying that they were suffering for the sins of their fathers—II Kings 23.26 singles out the sins of King Manasseh in particular—so that they, who had suffered defeat and exile were innocent sons of guilty fathers and grandfathers. Many chapters of Ezekiel are devoted to the endeavour to bring home the truth of the individual's personal responsibility. The lesson seems to have been so well learnt that it became something of a dogma that virtue would always bring its reward in this life, and that if a person was visited with great sufferings, that was proof that he was a great sinner.

[1] Ezek. 18.20.

47

This is what Job's three friends say to him, in the dialogue in the Book of Job; indeed, it is part of the primary purpose of that book to challenge this too comfortable dogma. Job indignantly replies that he is not a wicked man in the sense that they suggest; the solution must lie, somehow, on a deeper level. Job cannot find the answer; it comes only when the Lord Himself breaks into the dialogue and speaks to Job. On the human level, Job has been right in repudiating the narrow orthodoxy of his friends; but when he is confronted with the Lord Himself, he has to confess that he has uttered that which he understood not, things too high and too wonderful for him, that he knew not.[1] It was one thing to protest against their accusation, and another thing to seek to justify himself before God.

The same dogma is rejected in several psalms and in the Servant-poems in Isaiah, where the Servant of the Lord is seen suffering. Men shake their heads at him, and think he is suffering for his sins; but no, it is for their sins that he suffers, and it is through the sufferings of the Servant that the promised divine salvation is at last to come.[2]

Yet the dogma persisted. There was the Law of God for man to keep, and the Law marked out the way of righteousness. It seems right to say that in the period after Ezra the lesson that Israel was specially set to learn was the way of self-discipline in obedience to God's known will. But such a praiseworthy faithfulness involved the deadly peril of self-righteousness, as the godly compared themselves with those others around them who so lamentably departed from the Law and the Covenant. Such were the Pharisees of our Lord's day; and we ought not to be unjust to them, nor under-rate their real godliness and devotion.[3] We should rather see their peril as our own.

It is not till our Lord comes that this problem of man's self-righteousness can be solved. To Him, the self-righteous Pharisee presents a harder problem than the publican or sinner who knows his guilt. Nor are His disciples, or we Christians, allowed any shred of self-justification. When Peter seems to be claiming

---

[1] Job 42. 3.   [2] Isa. 53. 10–12.
[3] See, for this, T. W. Manson, *The Sayings of Jesus*, pp. 162–3.

for himself a species of merit, in saying 'Lo, we have left all, and followed Thee',[1] he receives his reproof in the words, 'Many shall be last that are first, and first that are last'.[2] If Peter takes credit to himself for his faithful discipleship, he will find one day that publicans and sinners are going into the Kingdom of God before him. A parable of God's grace follows.[3]

Here, as so often, St Paul is our Lord's best interpreter. The Parable of the Pharisee and the Publican is the key to the understanding of the argument of Romans, that 'by the works of the Law shall no flesh be justified'. And yet St Paul finds his grounds for criticizing the Old Testament in the Old Testament itself. If he could read in Leviticus 'He that doeth (the commandments) shall live in them',[4] he could also read 'Blessed is he whose unrighteousness is forgiven, and his sin covered'.[5] Here is the point which comes always as a paradox in discussions on ethics; the blessedness of being forgiven. In Exodus the Lord is represented as saying, 'I will not justify the wicked';[6] the paradox is seen in the fact that when St Paul in Romans speaks of God as 'Him that justifieth the ungodly',[7] his words in the Greek are the direct contradiction of the text in Exodus according to the Greek Bible.

Here, then, we have a problem stated in the Old Testament which cannot be solved till Christ has brought the answer by His death and resurrection. The Old Testament wrestles with the difficulty, and states it by giving expression to partial truths which can sometimes be dangerously one-sided. As Dr A. M. Ramsey, the present Archbishop of York, has expressed it: 'The faith of Israel did not drop down in a neat pattern from heaven, but was wrought out in the ups and downs of a turbulent history'.[8] Hence we are liable to get wrong answers out of the Bible if we take the Old Testament by itself without regard to its fulfilment in the New.[9]

---

[1] Matt. 19. 27.   [2] Matt. 19. 30.   [3] Matt. 20. 1–16.   [4] Gal. 3. 12; Lev. 18. 5.
[5] Rom. 4. 7; Ps. 32.1.   [6] Ex. 23. 7.   [7] Rom. 4. 5.
[8] A. M. Ramsey, *The Glory of God and the Transfiguration of Christ*, 1949, p. 21.
[9] Illustrations of this can be found in G. E. Phillips, *The Old Testament and the World Church*, Lutterworth, 1942, drawn from the teaching and the use of the Bible in the Younger Churches. See pp. 8–9 and other instances in the first three chapters.

(ii) *The tendency to Nationalism.* As Israel, having the Law of God, was tempted to legalism, so, being the People of God, she was tempted to a wrong nationalism. Here, too, the temptation is held in check by the fact that the Lord God is the Judge of His people; and it is only in the New Testament that the problem receives its final answer.

This matter is one that is of urgent and world-wide importance to-day. As it comes in the Bible, it is a large and complicated question; but as in the case of legalism, only a brief and summary statement can be given here.

First, we have the simple and unsophisticated nationalism of the period of the Judges and the early monarchy. It is taken for granted that the enemies of Israel are the Lord's enemies; the Lord's servants such as Samuel and David, show a fierce, even a ferocious zeal against them, and they are not blamed for it. Later, the time comes when Israel herself is denounced by the prophets as set under the Lord's judgment, and they can even speak of the Lord fighting against Jerusalem. Israel has to suffer under this judgment, in her complete political ruin. But the same prophets see the oppressing nations, who execute the Lord's judgment on Israel, as themselves subject to His judgment.[1]

Thus the Lord God is the universal King, the Judge of all the nations; shall He not at last make His kingly rule actual over all nations, over man whom He has created? Here is one of the great themes of the Bible, indeed the central theme of the Bible: the Kingdom or kingly rule or reign of God. Such a Kingdom there shall be; and Israel, His chosen People, is to be His instrument. By her suffering in the Exile she is being fitted for her vocation; she is to be the penitent nation of the future New Covenant, having repented of her past unfaithfulness to God. Sometimes in the Servant-poems it seems that Israel herself is the Servant of the Lord;[2] through her all nations are to come to know and serve the Lord God.

But how shall this be? Various answers are given, partly

---

[1] See, for instance, Isa. 10. 5–15 (Assyria); Jer. 50. 22–3 (Babylon).
[2] As in Isa. 49. 3.

different, partly complementary. (a) Sometimes it is plainly said that all nations are to come and share in the knowledge of God which Israel has received, and come with her to worship Him.[1] (b) Sometimes it seems that Israel, so cruelly humiliated in the Exile, is to receive a compensating glory, and the other nations are to serve her, bringing back the scattered Israelites to their homeland. So it is in the great chapter, Isa. 60, where it is not said that the nations are to share in Israel's privileges; they are content to behold God's glory thus manifested. (c) There is also to be God's Judgment on all nations, which sometimes is seen as complete destruction, sometimes as chastisement. In Obadiah vv. 10–16 there is judgment on the Edomites for their cruelty to the suffering Israelites at the time of the Fall of Jerusalem. Very notable also is the judgment pronounced on Tyre and on Egypt for their insolent and godless pride.[2]

In the last two centuries before Christ, the attempt of Antiochus Epiphanes to introduce a uniform Greek culture throughout his dominions led to a deliberate attempt to crush Israel's faith and worship out of existence. This called forth a twofold reaction: the patient faithfulness of the Maccabean martyrs, whose praises are celebrated in Heb. 11.34–8, and on the other hand the successful holy war waged by Judas Maccabaeus. This latter set the pattern of the hope of the coming Kingdom which was fixed in the middle of the first century B.C. in the *Psalms of Solomon*, and was held by the dominant Pharisaic party in our Lord's day. Here again the two strains appear: the godly Pharisees, who prayed and fasted, setting their hopes on a divine intervention, and the Zealots, anxious to settle matters by the sword; but common to both was the hope of a coming Kingdom of Israel, in which she would be set free from the oppressing Roman power, and the Gentiles would be subject to her.

Then 'the word of God came to John' the Baptist; he was mighty in the Scriptures and struck a note that had not been heard for some time: that Israel herself was subject to the Lord's

[1] As in Isa. 45. 22–3; Ps. 86. 9–10, and many other places.
[2] See Ezek. 28, 2; 29. 2 (Tyre); and 29. 3 (Egypt).

judgment.[1] He was bringing back the word spoken by the old prophets.

Then came our Lord. He rejected altogether the idea of a Messiah exercising political power, as a temporal king. Therefore in His ministry He is found avoiding the titles of Christ (Messiah) and Son of David; He does not wholly reject them, but calls Himself by preference Son of Man, making a plain reference thereby[2] to Daniel with its prophecy of a divine Kingdom that is to be universal.[3] Yet His mission is to Israel; for He must go to the centre, to restore and heal Israel, the People of God, that she may fulfil her vocation to bring the knowledge of God to all nations.[4] He knows that the cost of this will be His death; He accepts this, and prophesies His death and resurrection.

Through His death and resurrection it comes to pass. Within a few years Gentiles are being admitted to a share in Israel's privileges; they become 'children of Abraham'.[5] Israel is now no longer one nation; she is enlarged to include all nations. The Law and the prophets are not destroyed, but are fulfilled. Henceforth in the Church of God 'there is neither Jew nor Greek';[6] though the racial differences remain, they are brought together into a new unity which God has made. There is no place now for any exclusive nationalism, dominating and oppressing. All national cultures are now to find their place within the new Unity.

Here then is another problem which the Old Testament was unable to solve, and to which it gave some imperfect answers. Yet the Old Testament writers themselves were looking forward to the messianic future; and it is only in the light of the fulfilment of that messianic hope which came in Christ that the Old Testament can rightly be interpreted.

(iii) Our third point, *the vindictive psalms*, is really a corollary fo the second.

---

[1] Luke 3. 3, 7–9.   [2] Mark 14. 62.   [3] Dan. 7. 13–14.
[4] See for this my book *The Throne of David*, 1941, pp. 92–6 and Chap. IX, pp. 211 ff.
[5] Gal. 3. 29.   [6] Gal. 3. 28.

The psalmists often pray quite vindictively for vengeance on the Lord's enemies; and the same note is heard in the prophets, especially in Jeremiah, possibly the saintliest of them all. To us Anglicans, these psalms present a special problem, because we recite the whole psalter in our daily morning and evening prayer; but they are a problem for all Christians, as being part of Scripture. To the Liberals, it seemed that these psalms were simply sub-Christian and unfit for use in our worship. 'It was said, Thou shalt love thy neighbour, and hate thine enemy: but I say into you, Love your enemies.'[1] Even in time of war, or rather, most of all in time of war, we must not hate our enemies, or forget that they are people with whom after the war we must live in peace. Therefore, in the Revised Prayer Book proposed in 1928, a number of verses in the psalms were printed in brackets, with liberty to omit them.

But it is not right to deal thus with Holy Scripture; and the difficulty concerns not these psalms only, but much else in the Old Testament. Our Lord came not to destroy but to fulfil the Old Testament; and to cut out parts of psalms is to 'destroy', and to do so in a bungling way.

There is a better way. It is to see how our Lord actually does 'fulfil' the Old Testament in this particular instance. We must ask the question, Who are the Lord's enemies? In the period of the Judges, and after, it was taken for granted that the Lord's enemies were the enemies of Israel, and the Israelites acted accordingly. Then came the time when the prophets denounced the sins of Israel, and pictured the enemy who was about to attack Jerusalem as 'the rod of his wrath';[2] and there was a continual conflict of the 'true prophets' against such false prophets as Hananiah, Jeremiah's adversary, and other false Israelites, betrayers of Israel's faith, deniers of the Covenant. Who were the Lord's enemies now? Surely these, the ungodly in Israel.

And here we are at the 'cursing psalms'. The Lord's servant, the psalmist, has his back to the wall; he is maintaining God's cause, his one desire is for His honour to be vindicated and for

[1] Matt. 5. 43-4.   [2] Isa. 10. 5.

that which is right to be done. He is hard pressed; and he prays that God's enemies may be brought to nought, punished, destroyed. Does any personal vindictiveness against these enemies come into it? Maybe; but we are not in a position to pronounce judgment on him. Certainly it is the Lord's cause that he supremely cares about.

Then comes our Lord. In His words we find the most terrible words of wrath against sin in the whole Bible.[1] And yet we hear Him praying, as they nail Him to the cross, 'Father, forgive them'; He has accepted that cross and passion because He is identified with Israel, the People of God; He must bear their sins, for He is come to redeem them. Who are the Lord's enemies now? Now at last we are in sight of the answer. The Lord's enemies are not those poor misguided people, whom Satan has beguiled into sin, and whom He has come to deliver; not they, but Satan and the hosts of evil who have beguiled and ruined them. Our Lord's wrath can indeed blaze out against men when they deliberately identify themselves with evil and harden their hearts;[2] but the real enemies are those of whom St Paul speaks: 'Our wrestling', he says, 'is not against flesh and blood (i.e. human enemies), but against the principalities and powers . . . the spiritual hosts of wickedness in celestial places.'[3]

Father Benson of Cowley, in his book *The War-songs of the Prince of Peace*, gives to one of these 'cursing psalms' the heading 'The Wrath of the Lamb'. There is a wrath of the Son of God against all evil in devils and in men who sell themselves to do evil and exclude God from their lives; and it is this wrath that we should have in mind when we use these psalms, and in particular His wrath against our own sins. All religion that leaves out the wrath of God and the fear that is due to Him, is false religion.

It was this wrath that the psalmist was seeking to express, though the time had not yet come when that wrath was 'revealed', as it is now.[4] In his time the issue of the conflict of

---

[1] See in St. Mark's Gospel, 3. 29; 9. 42; 14. 21.
[2] Mark 3.5.   [3] Eph. 6.12 ff.   [4] Rom. 1. 18.

God with evil was not fully clear; it is made fully clear only in Christ. Here then we have one more instance of the imperfection of the Old Testament apart from Christ. We must see the Bible as a whole. We must see the truth of the Bible as fully expressed only in Christ. As Hudson Taylor wrote in his little book on the Song of Solomon 'The Incarnate Word is the true key to the written Word.'[1]

We have seen in this chapter that in three important instances the Old Testament can lead us to give wrong answers to present-day questions when it is taken by itself and interpreted without regard to its fulfilment in the New Testament. It seems clear, then, that any rigid doctrine of the Inerrancy of the Bible is again too narrow to fit the facts. We shall see in the next chapter that such a rigid doctrine, known as the 'dictation-theory' of Inspiration, has been widely held in the Church, as indeed Dr Sasse has reminded us in the quotation which we made in the first chapter[2]; and we shall also see that such a 'mechanical' view of Inspiration is repudiated by the responsible Evangelical leaders.

Yet it is in itself paradoxical to assert that the Book of God's Truth contains error. We shall go on to examine this paradox in the following chapters, and we shall see that the solution of the paradox must lie in a deeper consideration of the words 'truth' and 'error'. In the Anglican Litany we pray God to 'bring into the way of truth all such as have erred and are deceived'; plainly this sort of error is not to be attributed to the Bible. But there are other sorts of error which are relatively trivial. The all-important point is that there are various *levels* of truth and therefore also of error.

[1] *Union and Communion* (China Inland Mission and Lutterworth Press), p. 2.
[2] p. 12 above.

V

God's Truth and Human Formulations

IN the last chapter it was argued that the formula of the Inerrancy of Scripture is too narrow to cover the facts, either of the character of the various writings, or of the admitted imperfection of the Old Testament in relation to the New. The doctrine of Inerrancy is however held by conservative evangelicals to be substantially true in a broad and general way, and is distinguished by them from the rigid doctrine that Holy Scripture must be taken to be entirely free from error in every detail. This rigid view coincides with the 'dictation-theory' of Inspiration, that the human writer was a pen with which the Holy Spirit wrote.

This dictation-theory is to the best of my belief repudiated by all the conservative evangelical leaders, because it leaves no room for the individuality of the human writers. It is not necessary therefore in this book to deal with it in detail, or to give a history of it. But something must be said about it, because it was the prevailing view in the Church for many centuries. It would be too much, probably, to say that the Roman Catholic Church is officially committed to it, though the phrase quoted from the Vatican Council Decree on p. 34 above, that the Scriptures 'have God as their author' (*Deum habent auctorem*), and the phrase 'by dictation of the Holy Spirit' (*Spiritu Sancto dictante*) quoted in the previous sentence from the Council of Trent,[1] come dangerously near it. It would seem that this dictation-theory is held by sects such as Jehovah's Witnesses, the Seventh Day Adventists, and the British Israelites.

This dictation-theory, that the human writer was passive under the influence of the Holy Spirit, was widely held in the

[1] Denzinger, *Enchiridion*, §§ 1787 and 783.

under the influence of the Holy Spirit, was widely held in the early Church, and many of the Fathers became entangled in it.[1] Athenagoras, about A.D. 170, described the prophets as speaking in ecstasy, with the Holy Spirit speaking through them like a flute-player playing on a flute (*Legatio pro Christianis* 9); and Pseudo-Justin says the same in *Cohortatio ad Graecos* 8. Gregory the Great describes the writers as the pen (*calamus*) of the Holy Spirit, so that it is ridiculous to inquire into the authorship of the Epistles; for 'since we hold the Holy Spirit to be the author, we do nothing else if we inquire into the authorship than to inquire, when we read a letter, about the pen with which it was written'.[2] Where did these ideas come from?

They came partly from Jewish sources. According to the legend in II Esdras 14. 22–40 (one of the books of our Apocrypha) the whole text of the Old Testament Scriptures, having been lost in the Exile, was revealed to Ezra, who in forty days dictated to his scribes the twenty-four canonical books, besides seventy apocryphal writings. There is also the late Jewish legend that the seventy-two translators of the Greek Bible had independently produced an identical version, proving thereby that the Holy Spirit had inspired them all. (Yet the *Letter of Aristeas* had given a very different account; the translators had worked together in one building, and through mutual collation had agreed on the wording.) It was Philo who had set forth the idea that inspiration was a state of ecstatic enthusiasm which can only fall to the lot of the sage,[3] 'for he alone is a sounding-instrument of God, invisibly played and struck by Him'. On this the German scholar H. Leisegang comments, 'With these words Philo demonstrates his complete misunderstanding of Old Testament prophecy'.

But this idea of inspiration came ultimately from pagan sources. It was just in this way that the Delphic oracle was held to be inspired. The pagan world knew prophetic ecstasy. In Virgil's *Aeneid*, Book VI, we have the description of the Cumaean

---

[1] For this and the next four paragraphs I am following Dr Herman Sasse's article 'Sacra Scriptura' in the *Reformed Theological Review*, Melbourne, from which a quotation has been made on p. 12 above.

[2] *Preface to Morals*, i. 2., Migne *P.L.* lxxv. col. 371.

[3] *Quis rerum divinarum heres*, 259.

Sibyl; later came the Sibylline Oracles, and some of the Fathers speak of revelation in the Hebrew prophets and the Sibyls as wonderfully in harmony.[1] The Apologists fell into this snare because they were seeking to explain the Inspiration of Scripture to pagans, and in so doing accepted from their opponents the form in which the question was stated; hence in trying to give a right answer to a wrongly-stated question they failed to give the answer which they ought to have given. There was a world of difference between saying that the Holy Spirit had *dictated* to the writer what he must say, and saying that the Holy Spirit had *suggested* certain things to his recollection.

From this confusion even the great Augustine was unable to escape. He is found hovering between the ideas of 'dictation' and 'suggestion', and he comes down mostly on the side of 'dictation', so that even in the smallest details the principle must be valid that the Bible is free from all mistakes, inaccuracies, and contradictions.[2] Accepting the later Jewish legend about the composition of the Septuagint, against Jerome who vigorously repudiated it,[3] he laboured to reconcile the Hebrew text of Jonah 3.4, where the prophet announces the destruction of Nineveh within forty days, and the LXX which makes it 'three days', and he found an answer in making the two texts into an allegory of the Saviour who lay for three days in the tomb and communed with the apostles for forty days;[4] so one Spirit had spoken through both versions of the text. Similarly he explained the discrepancy between the synoptic and Johannine datings of the Cleansing of the Temple by supposing that it was cleansed several times,[5] and the discrepancy between Mark's statement that our Lord was crucified at the third hour,[6] and that of John that Pilate delivered Him up for crucifixion at the sixth hour,[7] by saying that 'Mark judged most truly that the Lord's murderer was

---

[1] This left its mark on patristic and mediaeval hymnody, as in the sequences *Laetabundi* and *Dies Irae*, which appear in the *English Hymnal*, Nos. 22 and 351.
[2] *Ep.* 82.
[3] 'I do not know who was the first writer to construct by his falsehood those seventy cells at Alexandria, in which men separated from one another wrote an identical version', says Jerome in his *Apologia adversus libros Rufini*, ii.25.
[4] *City of God*, xviii.44.   [5] *De consensu evangelistarum*, ii.67.
[6] Mark 15.25.   [7] John 19.14.

rather the tongue of the Jews than the hand of the soldiers.'[1]
But this is no explanation of the discrepancy. Again, in Matt.
27.9 a quotation which is really from Zachariah is attributed to
Jeremiah. On this text St Jerome said that St Matthew 'errs in
the name', but that it was his business 'not to chase after words
and syllables, but to explain sentences concerning doctrine';[2]
St Augustine discusses it at length, and concludes that it was
an error of memory, which he would have corrected later,
had he not reflected that the falsity of his memory, aided by the
Holy Spirit, would not have occurred unless it had been God's
will that the text should so read'.[3]

Dr Sasse says, with regard to this text, that 'Origen, if we are
to trust Rufinus' translation—otherwise the statement would
have to stand to the credit of Rufinus alone—indicates that this
is an error of the Scripture (*errorem scripturae*—Migne, *P.G.* xiii
1709)'. He concludes the paper which I have been summarizing
by a reference to St John Chrysostom, the sage of the eastern
Church, who, he says, points the way to a better answer to the
problem of Inspiration by his doctrine of the *synkatabasis* or
'condescension' of God; commenting on Gen. 3.8 (the Lord
God walking in the garden in the cool of the day), he says that
'here the Scripture shows great humility (*tapeinotēs*) of speech'.[4]
Here, says Dr Sasse, 'a new doctrine of Holy Scripture begins to
become manifest, which, to use Luther's terms, is no longer a
theologia gloriae but a *theologia crucis;* a doctrine in which the
gracious condescension of God in Holy Scripture becomes a
parallel to the Incarnation of the Eternal Word, because He
who is the Word, is the content and the Lord of the Bible'.

To this it may be added that the corollary of the dictation-
theory of Inspiration is an intellectualist view of Revelation,
since that which is revealed by God consists of a written word.
To this corresponds the characteristically Latin view of Faith as
primarily an assent of the mind to the truth which has been
revealed; to believe *that* something is true. But the Biblical
meaning of Faith is primarily to believe *in* God, or in Christ;

[1] Ibid., ii.67.   [2] Jerome, *Ep.* 57.   [3] *De cons. ev.*, iii.7. 30.
[4] Migne, *P.G.* liii.135.

faith expresses a relation to a personal God. We shall pick these points up again a little later.

Archdeacon T. C. Hammond's little book *Inspiration and Authority*[1] is one that is widely read and highly valued among conservative evangelicals, and can be called a thoroughly representative book. What line does he take about Inspiration?

He altogether disavows any 'mechanical view of Inspiration'. 'If God intended to deliver a mechanical message, it seems obvious to reason that He would have employed mechanical means. If man can teach a parrot to talk, and can reproduce the sounds of the human voice by means of a revolving disc, God, it is to be assumed, could deliver a message of mere words, without soul or mind behind them. But the Scripture record assures us that God spoke through men. There is little of ecstasy or trance associated with inspired messages, although they are not wholly absent, since these also are part of human experiences. The Divine message was formulated under the guidance of God in those conditions which are incidental to the development of human thought. It may be assumed that there were real ideas and rational processes behind the utterances of the prophets, just as there are real ideas and rational processes behind the utterances of ordinary men. The Divine influence rendered these ideas peculiarly exalted and adequate to that conception of God which, within the limitations of our finite humanity and any further limitation of age and actual development, man was enabled to grasp and to hold.'[2] It is interesting to see how he avoids the pitfalls into which the early Christian apologists fell, mechanical inspiration and the association of inspiration with ecstasy; and how he leaves a real place for the individuality of the writers.

Again, the textual variations in the Scriptures do not present any serious problem, for in all important matters there is essential agreement:[3] 'the message of God has been preserved in verbal form with substantial accuracy'.[4] 'Nor is there much difficulty in the varying accounts of our Lord's words in the

[1] Published by I.V.F.; Inter-Varsity papers, No. 3. Its author was Principal of Moore College, Sydney, from 1936 to 1953.
[2] Ibid., p. 23. [3] Ibid., p. 35. [4] Ibid., p. 37.

four Gospel narratives', for the evangelists are not 'newspaper verbatim reporters'.[1]

He asserts 'verbal inspiration'; but this surely is not in itself a phrase that need be quarrelled with. For, if Scripture is inspired at all, it must be its words that are inspired; much as in a poem, the words which the poet has used are those which he has chosen to express his meaning, and it is only through the words that we know the poet's mind.[2] So Dr Hammond says, 'If all God's teachers had heard only unspeakable words there would have been no Bible'.[3] Hence he rejects the popular saying that 'the men indeed were inspired but not their utterances'.[4]

God's revelation, then, is transmitted to us in the Holy Scriptures by means of language.[5] Through language men communicate their thoughts one to another, and 'the success of any communication depends on the adequacy of the expression'.[6] 'It is therefore in accordance with the analogy of human experience that God should graciously employ those media which have proved the only effective instruments for the communication of thought'.[7]

But does this emphasis, right so far as it goes, on revelation through the written word lead to an over-emphasis on the intellectual aspect of revelation? I desire at this point to present an analysis of our ways of thought, with which I am sure that Dr Hammond and his friends will cordially agree, though it leads, as it seems to me, to a somewhat different conception of revelation from his. I express it in a schematic form derived from a familiar modern terminology, which depends on the use of the grammatical nominative and accusative cases.

(i) *I – it.* 'I' say something about 'it'; and 'it' can be my typewriter, or a flower in the garden, or the moon, or any other neuter (inanimate) thing. Thus 'I – it' can stand for all our knowledge about Things, and all *natural science*.

I – him. Now we have a masculine (or feminine) pronoun, denoting a person. I am talking about Edward, praising him

---

[1] Ibid., pp. 35, 36.
[2] Cf. for this point, my book, *The Authority of the Old Testament*, 1947, p. 24-5.
[3] *Inspiration and Authority*, p. 17.   [4] Ibid., p. 17.
[5] Ibid., pp. 11, 12.   [6] Ibid., p. 13.   [7] Ibid., p. 14.

perhaps, or else pulling his character to pieces; or I am writing his biography. Or (*I – them*) I am talking or writing about the Scottish nation, or about the communists. Here, then, we have *biography* and *history*.

I – Him. Here the capital letter stands for God. I am thinking or writing about God. The biblical writers continually thus speak of God in the third person. The co-ordinated statement of what we believe about God is *systematic theology*, which never goes beyond this use of the third person.

(ii) *I – thee*. Now my words are addressed to a person, to Edward. I may be praising him, or I may be telling him his faults; but he is there, listening, and he and I are in communication. Or I am writing to him; here we have a *letter*, addressed to a person.

I – Thee. Again the capital letter denotes God. I am praising Him, praying to Him. This is the language of *prayer*; 'we – Thee' is the language of *liturgy*, which is common prayer. But still it is the 'I' or the 'we', addressing God. (It is interesting at this point to note how Psalm 119 begins with 'I – Him', but at verse 4 passes to 'I – Thee', and so continues for the remaining 173 verses.)

(iii) *I – thou*. The small letter denotes my fellow-man; but now there are two nominatives. I am speaking to him, and he is answering. I am telling Edward what I think of him, and he is getting his own back. Or it may be that the 'thou' is a judge in a law-court, and he is sentencing me to be hanged. (Here we see that the question whether capital punishment ought to be retained is a very different question for the prisoner who is being condemned, from what it is in 'dispassionate' and 'objective' discussions on criminology.)

I – Thou. Here I am confronted with God, not merely as the Object of my thought, but as the Subject—with Him who called me into existence when I did not exist; who for me and for my salvation came down from heaven, and who loved me and gave Himself for me; who is my Judge now, and will be manifested as my Judge at the last day. Here the reality of God is seen in startling contrast with all our human thoughts about Him.

In this scheme, it will be noticed that (a) Things which we know by our sense-perception and analytical study (*I – it*) are on a lower level of existence than we, so that we can give what we call an 'objective' account of them. But (b) our fellow-men, about whom we express our judgments in speech and writing of history (*I – him* and also *I – thee* and *I – thou*), are on the same level as we; consequently, though it is part of our responsibility that we should form our judgments about them, we are forbidden[1] to pronounce any final judgment, since we are fellow-sinners with them. And (c) God, about whom we speak and express our doctrines (*I – Him*), to whom we pray (*I –Thee, we – Thee*), and who is our Maker, our Saviour and our Judge (*I – Thou, we – Thou*), is on a level infinitely above us.

Here we see in a clear light the difference between the Word of God and the words of men. The Word of God is God speaking and acting. The words of men are the human rendering of what we believe to be true about Him and His world. Can we then say, with Archdeacon Hammond, that the words of Scripture are 'adequate' to convey God's revelation? In one sense yes; for through the written word of Scripture God has spoken and still speaks. In another sense no; for no human words, not even those of Scripture, can convey to us, with our limited understanding, the whole glory of God.

And because the Word of God surpasses the power of human thought and language to comprehend it and express it fully, the work of Christ is described in the New Testament by means of paradoxes, which are often logically self-contradictory. Here are a few instances. 'God was in Christ reconciling the world to himself'; and here a purblind logic can make merry with the contradiction involved in the idea of God taking away His own wrath. 'God justifies the ungodly'; the Epistle to the Romans was written to elucidate the paradox that the righteous God justifies and saves sinful man. Christ is absent ('It is expedient for you that I go away') and is present ('Lo, I am with you alway'). We are God's children, and yet in danger of falling away ('We are become partakers of Christ, *if* we hold fast the

[1] Matt. 7.1.

beginning of our confidence firm unto the end').[1] Our resurrection-body will be the same and yet different; 'we shall be changed'[2] in a manner which we are not now able to comprehend; and the same difficulty comes in the Easter-narratives, with regard to our Lord's risen body, which is visible and tangible, but appears and disappears and is not subject to ordinary physical laws.

And so, the revelation of God in Scripture is not expressed in a systematic theology, but rather by means of pictures and images. Our Lord is the King, yet wields no temporal power; the Son of Man (Son of Adam); the Son of God, yet not as one of the many 'sons of God', but as the Only (*agapētos*) Son; He is the Head of His body which is the Church, the Bridegroom, the High-priest and the Victim, the Shepherd, the Physician,[3] the Fisherman,[4] the Sower, the final Judge. He speaks in parables; and the word 'parable' as it is used in Mark 3.23, 7.17, is a saying which expresses to those who have ears to hear 'the Mystery of the Kingdom of God', or in other words 'the Secret of the Advent of divine Majesty'. That is why His parables are for the disciples, to whom is given the mystery of the Kingdom of God,[5] while they remain 'parables' to those who are like the uncomprehending multitudes in Isaiah's day, not having eyes to see or ears to hear the Word of God.[6]

So it is that throughout Scripture the Word of God is conveyed often by means other than those of plain historical statement; by poetry and by tales, such as the story of Adam and Eve, through the symbolism of the sacrifices, and in the sacraments of the New Covenant. All these in their various ways speak the Word on a deeper level than that of logically reasoned argument or historical narrative.

Yet there must be systematic theology. Its function is to rationalize and co-ordinate the imagery in which the revelation is conveyed; and it is necessary because the imagery may easily be misinterpreted. So it was when the Arians argued that since every father is prior in time to his son, therefore there was a

---

[1] Heb. 3.14.   [2] I Cor. 15.51.   [3] Mark 2.17.   [4] Mark 1.17.
[5] Mark 4. 11–12.   [6] Isa. 6.9–10.

time when the Son of God did not exist. In this case the image of the Son needs to be correlated with that of the Word which God eternally utters.[1] It is the important duty of the systematic theologian to translate Biblical Theology into Dogmatic Theology. But systematic theology, though it is occupied throughout with the Word of God, consists of words of men; and nothing is more important for the systematic theologian than that he should be aware of his limitations.

Does Archdeacon Hammond's statement fall short just here? He is presenting the revelation of God in Scripture as truth conveyed to our minds by intelligible words. And so it is, and the words are 'adequate' for their purpose. But he does not sufficiently stress the fact that they are also inadequate. We get an impression, or more than an impression, that both he and other evangelical theologians are too ready to pass straight from the written word of Scripture to a rationalized statement in a dogmatic theology; too ready to have answers for all questions, taken indeed out of Scripture, but still answers formulated by themselves. The danger in such a procedure is always that of neglecting other things said in Scripture; for the truth presented by Scripture is many-sided. There is no evangelical *Summa Theologica* like those of the scholastics; but there does appear nevertheless to be an evangelical orthodoxy, with an accepted set of answers for all the questions that are to be asked.

If I may give one instance, stress is regularly laid by the evangelical theologians on the propitiation of God's wrath in our Lord's work of atonement; Christ suffered for guilty man, He bore God's wrath, and by His death God's wrath was propitiated. We can indeed be thankful to these theologians for taking seriously the wrath of God and the fear that is due to Him,[2] for it is neglected in much theology and preaching today. But two complaints can in general be made: first, that these expositions of the Atonement regularly stop short with the

[1] John 1.1.
[2] So Leon Morris says in *The Apostolic Preaching of the Cross*, 1955, p. 156: 'The wrath of God is a conception which cannot be eradicated from the Old Testament without irreparable loss', and in his Ch. V shows that the same is true of the New Testament.

Death of Christ, and do not go on, as St Paul goes on, to Baptism and man's death to sin[1] and to the work of the Holy Spirit;[2] and second, that one type of atonement doctrine alone is set forth, that of neo-Protestant orthodoxy. But while this is for all serious students an important exposition of the Atonement, there are other expositions equally based on Scripture which also shed light on this central point of our faith.[3]

Earlier in this chapter[4] mention was made of the Latin view of faith as the assent of the mind to revealed truth, and the difference between 'believing in' God or Christ, and 'believing that' this or that doctrine is true. Evangelical theologians do not fall into the error of thus defining the word 'faith', for the testimony of the New Testament is very clear that faith is a personal response to the personal God. But there is the danger, when the revelation of God is seen as consisting of the written word, that the meaning of revelation will be interpreted in an intellectualist way, and the word 'faith' will not in practice be given its full meaning.

· There is indeed always an intellectual side to Faith: I cannot believe *in* God unless I know something *about* Him in whom I believe. So 'He that cometh *to* God must believe *that* he is, and that he is the rewarder of them that diligently seek Him'.[5] When we say in the creed that we believe in 'Jesus Christ His only Son our Lord', we immediately go on to the statements about His birth, His death and resurrection, His ascension and His eternal Kingdom. So it is in our common usage; I believe, having looked up the time-table, *that* the train for Melbourne will stop at our station at 7.52 p.m.; but I do not put faith *in* the train till I get into it and commit myself to it to carry me through the night to Melbourne. So faith *in* Christ presupposes

---

[1] Rom. 6. [2] Rom. 8.

[3] I am thinking of such expositions as Gustaf Aulén's *Christus Victor*, and still more of O. C. Quick's last book, *The Gospel of the New World*; as compared with Leon Morris, who in his important book just mentioned does not touch on the death to sin when he deals with man's reconciliation, and with T. C. Hammond's *In Understanding be Men*, 1936, a book which in many ways admirably fulfils its purpose as 'a Synopsis of Christian Doctrine for Non-theological Students', but in his fifteen pages on the Atonement he sets forth only the evangelical view, recommending for reading Dale, Denney, Hodge, and Griffith Thomas.

[4] p. 59. [5] Heb. 11.6.

right belief *about* Him, but is far wider and deeper; it is a response which includes trust and self-oblation to a Person, whose word given to us in the gospels is to be obeyed, and whose presence is known in the sacraments, the signs and the means of His personal action.

He is the Word of God, who for us men and for our salvation was made man. And here the problem of the Word of God and human words meets us at the highest point of all. He is true man, and in His life on earth He spoke human words. His human knowledge was true human knowledge. Was He, as man, omniscient, carrying in His human mind the fulness of divine knowledge about the whole universe and all men? We must say No; for this would be to deny that He was true man, made like to us in all things, yet without sin.[1] Yet we must say that in Him as man dwelt the fulness of divine wisdom; all theories of His 'emptying' of Himself[2] which suppose that in becoming man He left His divine nature behind, to resume it at His ascension, are contrary to the Faith. We must say, somehow, that in His human nature God was present and was revealed; in Him were God's Righteousness and God's Truth, God's Love and God's Wrath, translated (so to speak) into our human language.

Then what about His human knowledge? We are bound to say that in the days of His boyhood He was a real human boy, and that in the synagogue school He learnt His lessons with the other boys; nor can we think that when He was grown up He could have conversed at any moment in Sanskrit or Chinese. James Orr[3] stated this point well: 'No one who thinks seriously on the subject will maintain that during His earthly life Jesus carried in His consciousness a knowledge of all events of history, past, present and future, of all arts and sciences, including the results of our modern astronomies, geologies, biologies, mathematics, of all languages, etc. To suppose this would be to annul the reality of His human consciousness entirely. The Incarnation means that Jesus, in becoming man, entered into all the conditions of a true human life, growth and development included.

---

[1] Heb. 4.15.   [2] *kenosis*, Phil. 2.7.
[3] James Orr, *Revelation and Inspiration*, Duckworth, 1910, p. 150.

. . . The limitations of His human consciousness were not assumed, but real.' He continues: 'Does this acknowledged limitation of the human knowledge of Christ, and ignorance of earthly science, imply *error* on the part of Jesus? This is a position which must as strongly be contested. Ignorance is not error, nor does the one thing necessarily imply the other. That Jesus should use the language of His time on things indifferent, where no judgment or pronouncement of His own was involved, is readily understood; that He should be the victim of illusion, or false judgment, on any subject on which He was called to pronounce, is a perilous assertion. . . . False judgment, where moral questions are involved, can hardly fail to issue in wrong action'.[1]

Thus we find Him declaring His ignorance of the day and hour of the Advent: 'Of that day or that hour knoweth no one, not even the angels in heaven, neither the Son, but the Father'.[2] Therefore it was discreditable when St Thomas Aquinas, following a tradition of interpretation dating from the Fathers, said that He did know but chose not to say.[3]

What is to be said then of His quotation of Ps. 110.1 as written by David?[4] Orr does not deal with this question in the passage from which I have been quoting, and I do not know what answer he gave. But he lays down this principle: 'It may readily be admitted that when Jesus used popular language about "Moses" and "Isaiah" He did nothing more than designate certain books, and need not be understood as giving *ex cathedra* judgments on the intricate critical questions which the contents of these books raise. Had such questions been proposed to Him for decision, He would probably have dealt with them as He did with the appeal about inheritance: "Man, who made me a judge or a divider over you"?'[5] As Orr said earlier, we ought not

---

[1] Ibid., pp. 150–1.
[2] Mark 13.32.
[3] *Summa Theologica*, III.x.2, reply to 1st objection. For the Fathers, see Gore, *Dissertations*, pp. 111–121 (1907 edition); Irenaeus accepts His human ignorance, also Clement, Origen; later Fathers are more doubtful, but the later Fathers from Ephraim Syrus and Cyril of Alexandria deny it (but not the Antiochene Theodoret), pp. 131 ff.
[4] Mark 12. 35–7.   [5] Ibid., p. 153.

to think of Him as being in error on any subject on which He was called upon to pronounce; and on what subject was He making a pronouncement on this occasion? Not on a critical question which is being asked now, but was not being asked then; but on the high theme of the nature and function of the Messiah. He was asserting that the Scribes, who looked for a Messiah holding temporal power, had not understood their own Scriptures which spoke of Him as seated at God's right hand.

We ought not then to invoke His authority as deciding for us the critical problem of the authorship of a psalm, as is done in the *New Bible Commentary* (I.V.F.) in the notes on the psalm and on Matthew, Mark and Luke. If it be maintained on purely critical grounds that Ps. 110 was written by David, as is done, I believe, by some Scandinavian scholars, that is another matter. But we must not invoke our Lord's authority to decide a question which He was not answering.

The knowledge which concerns merely factual information is one thing; the knowledge which is wisdom, understanding and insight, is quite another. Orr goes on to make this distinction, taking as instances first His belief in the reality of angels, of demons, of Satan: 'If language has any meaning, He unquestionably believed in a spiritual kingdom of evil whose power it was His mission to overthrow, and whose agency He recognized in the unhappy subjects of "possession". Surely also if there is any one thing in which Christ's intuition can be trusted, it is in a matter of this kind, which turns on *rapport* with the spiritual world.'[1] The second instance is His attitude to Holy Scripture; He 'unquestionably did believe in the Old Testament as the inspired record of God's revelations in the past—did believe in the essential historicity of its contents— did believe in the law—did believe that psalms and prophets pointed forward with unerring finger to Himself'.[2] We have seen how Dr Orr put in a different class from *this* belief in the Old Testament mere questions of date and authorship.

We can easily add to Orr's two instances; we can add all that our Lord says about God, and about Prayer, and about man's

[1] Ibid., p. 152.   [2] Ibid., p. 153.

life in relation to God. He 'knew what was in man', saw into the depths of human nature, discerned hypocrisy from true religion, saw the vanity of covetousness and pride; He saw the true relation of man and woman in marriage, and went straight to the Old Testament passages which proclaimed it;[1] He saw the duty which man owes to Caesar in relation to that which man owes to God. In matters such as these we have, throughout His recorded teaching, what might be called a 'translation' of the divine wisdom Itself into human terms; and this word 'translation' seems to give the essential idea, which may be illustrated from a translation of a Hebrew psalm into English, or the translation of the biblical teaching about our Lord's death for our sins into the language spoken in one of the Melanesian islands, and still more into the idiom in which a Melanesian islander thinks, or again into the idiom of a European dock labourer. Somewhat thus the words of our Lord are a rendering into our human language of the very Wisdom of God; and when He speaks of these universal things, His words are authoritative and final.

[1] Gen. 1.27; 2.24; quoted in Mark 10.6–8.

VI

The Truth of Science and of History

'IF a man sets forth the facts as he sees them, systematically marshalling the relevant evidence and argument, not attempting to persuade, but letting the facts themselves come through—that is *scientific* writing or speaking. But if he seeks to persuade men to believe something, consciously trying to win them to that belief, then he is engaging in *propaganda*. If he is trying to persuade them to do something, that is *agitation*. The scientist, the propagandist, the agitator, all engage in *publicity*. Advertising is agitation with a special objective. It seeks to make men buy things . . .'[1]

In the world to-day there is perhaps no class of men that receives so universal a tribute of respect as the scientists. We admire not only their astonishing knowledge and skill, each in his own department, but also and still more their single-minded and self-sacrificing devotion to truth. In astronomy, physics, geology, biology, the facts have to be discovered, often by incredibly accurate observation and measurement, and to be co-ordinated and understood by hypotheses and theories. But all the hypotheses are provisional, and are continually being pulled to pieces and reassembled as fresh facts appear or some new insight is gained. There is readiness to learn from one another, and to follow truth where it leads. It is only where there is war or the threat of war that scientific investigations are kept secret and their results jealously guarded.

Natural science is then 'catholic', in the proper sense of that word, in that it is true universally, for all men. There is not a Protestant or a Roman Catholic astronomy or archaeology, any more than there is an English or a German or an American

[1] From the *Current Affairs Bulletin*, Tutorial Classes Dept., Sydney University, 20th Feb., 1956, on 'Advertising'.

science of geology. The facts are the same for all; in being facts, they are God's facts. The theories are common property.

It is a cardinal principle in all scientific work that the conclusions of research cannot be dictated beforehand; they must emerge out of the facts and explain them. No scientist can allow his research to be interfered with by philosophical or theological dogmas which prescribe beforehand the conclusions that must be reached. This was the battle that Galileo and Kepler had to fight against the theologians and still more against the philosophers who sought to tie them down to the conclusions of Aristotelian physics and astronomy. Because the circle was the perfect figure, and God had created the world, therefore the planets must move in circular orbits. 'It was not a bishop but the Professor of Philosophy at Padua who refused to look through Galileo's telescope; and his colleague at Pisa tried, as Galileo said, by means of logical arguments "to charm the planets from the sky".'[1]

But Theology is always a puzzle to the scientific worker. He cannot understand a study which appears to have all its dogmas laid down in advance; for such procedure is contrary to his whole method. Natural Science has indeed suffered much interference from the theological side, and not only in those early days of three and four centuries ago when it had to fight and win its battles for freedom. The researches of Darwin into the mutation and evolution of species met with bitter opposition from many theologians; among these were the original fundamentalists, who were apt to condemn the works of the natural scientists, as we saw in chapter II, and to hail with glee the modifications made in the theory of evolution, as though these indicated that the scientific 'system' was breaking up. Whenever theologians do this, they are putting Theology into a false position.

Theology is indeed concerned with the facts studied by the natural sciences, but it approaches them from a different angle.

[1] From my book, *The Authority of the Old Testament*, 1947, p. 95; quotation from Basil Willey, *The Seventeenth Century Background*, 1934, p. 20.

Since it (Theology) deals with God as the Creator of the world and the Ground of all existence, it is related to all man's knowledge of the world and to all the sciences that there are; but it approaches their subject-matter from a different direction. The other sciences take each its own department of study, and pursue their investigations in their several departments, continually opening up new lines of research and extending the boundaries of our knowledge. But Theology is what has been called a "reversed science", approaching the subject-matter of the other sciences from the opposite direction'.[1] This 'opposite direction' is the interpretation of the physical order in the light of the purpose for which God created it, as made known in the revelation of God through Christ and in Scripture. Hence, while natural science starts as it were from below, with the facts given in our sense-experience, Theology endeavours to say what can rightly be said about the Glory of God as it is shown in His created universe. Thus the formula of the Old Testament prophets, 'Thus saith the Lord', is in a sense characteristic of Theology. Therefore there ought not to be any conflict between the scientist and the theologian. The theologian must go to school with the scientist to learn the physical explanation of the facts. He himself, starting from the revelation of the personal God, must endeavour to see these facts together with all the other facts of human life and history, in the light of God's revealed will and purpose.

Historical science is more difficult than natural science in this respect, that while natural science deals with physical facts $(I - it)$,[2] history deals with the actions and motives of men $(I - them)$, and it is difficult for the historian to attain objectivity, since he himself is part of history and an actor in it. Winston Churchill writes a history of the last war, having been himself a maker of that history; and the same is true in some degree of every historian, in so far as the nation or church to which he

---

[1] From my booklet, *Theology and Theological Study*, Angus and Robertson, Sydney, London, Melbourne and Wellington, 1955, p. 2. This was a lecture given in July of that year to the Melbourne College of Divinity.
[2] pp. 61–3, above.

belongs has in some measure shaped the events which he describes. An English and a German historian study European history from different angles; an Asian historian will again have a different perspective. Religious differences affect the writing of history even more deeply; there are Catholic and Protestant histories of the Reformation. Or again, Gibbon saw the decline and fall of the Roman Empire from his own eighteenth-century point of view; and histories written to-day from the undenominational point of view of the secular university present both ecclesiastical and other matters differently from the view of a Christian historian, who sees the ecclesiastical events as from the inside, and will have a partly different standard of judgment for the course of the events as a whole.

Such is the problem of historical interpretation. On the other side, there is in history the investigation of the factual course of events, where a decision must be reached solely on the basis of the evidence; and here the problem of history is similar to that of natural science. What were the facts about the Forged Decretals? Did Richard III murder the Princes in the Tower, or was the deed done by Henry VII or under his orders? Was Ps. 110 composed by David? Was the Law all written by Moses, as it stands in the Pentateuch, or was it slowly built up through many centuries till its last revision in the Priestly Code? Were the Pastoral Epistles as they stand written by St Paul? These are all questions of fact, and factual evidence only is admissible, as in the case of natural science. There is however the important difference that the facts are all concerned with persons, and the characters of the persons concerned and their religious beliefs have very much indeed to do with the right estimation of the factual evidence. With this proviso the principle stands; no external presuppositions, such as a doctrine of Inerrancy or the articles of the Christian Creed, can influence the estimate of the evidence. For the appeal of the Christian Faith is to the facts; the words of the Creed, 'suffered under Pontius Pilate' make this appeal to history, and involve the duty of honest historical investigation. This is absolutely demanded by the fact that the revelation of God took place through the divine action in history.

74

This principle must stand even in the central and crucial case of the resurrection of our Lord from death on the third day. It might seem that this is a case where, for Christians, the answer to a historical question is given beforehand; how can they make an honest inquiry into the evidence when they know the answer beforehand? We must deal with this problem very seriously; for this reason it will be convenient to hold over this point till the conclusion of this chapter.

In the science of history, fact and interpretation are closely related to one another; but they must be distinguished and so far as possible kept apart. The events happened as they did happen. But what is the standard of interpretation? Is it to be the humanistic outlook of the modern university? Is it to be the Marxian standard of irresistible economic forces? Is it to be the Christian outlook, and if so, can it be other than some denominational outlook? Yet if the objective and scientific character of Theology is properly understood, it is possible for at least some real approximation to be made to a 'catholic', that is to say, not a merely denominational view. If I may quote from my lecture at Melbourne, with reference to the study of church history:

'The theologian as historian must study the facts of his history like any other historian. His concern is specially with the history of the Church, and therefore with the religious history; but church history is bound up with the history of civilization, with the economics, politics, and everything. His task is to see with a prophet's eye the various situations as they arose, and the reactions both of churchmen and of other men to those situations. Thus in regard to the history of the Reformation, he must be asking what were the sins of the mediaeval church, and what was the judgment of God passed in the course of the history upon those sins, and what were the insights and the failures of the Reformers on the one side and of the Counter-Reformation on the other; what were the works of the Holy Ghost, what were the shortcomings due to human frailty and human sin. He must strive to be impartial and see things as they were; but he is not infallible, he sees the events from a Catholic or a Protestant viewpoint, and he is in no position to pronounce the final judgment which belongs to God alone. Yet he is responsible, as a theologian, for giving a true interpretation, so far as his powers extend, of the meaning of the history.'[1]

We have now reached the point at which an endeavour must be made to estimate the strength and the weakness of Liberal Theology and Biblical Criticism. In Chapter II a rapid sketch was given of the Liberal Theology of about the year 1910, as it appeared to the original Fundamentalists, who rejected primarily its theological outlook and went on to reject its critical positions.

The glory of Liberalism was first its sustained endeavour to seek the truth of the events, just as the natural scientists were seeking the truth about natural phenomena. The Liberals knew that the facts, whatever they were, were God's facts; that all truth is God's truth; that in all the investigations of natural science men were learning part of God's glory as it is revealed in His works. Therefore the real facts also of the biblical history and of the composition of the documents must be ascertained. The religion of the Old Testament must be compared with the new knowledge that was being gained about the other religions of the world. Above all, the story must be seen as a truly human story, and the actors in it as real men.

Therefore the Holy Spirit was not absent in this new study of the Bible. This was recently proclaimed in an Oxford University sermon by C. F. Evans: 'Must we not claim that the same Holy Spirit, who spake by the prophets and who inspired the Scriptures, does in another and a lesser mode of His operation lead men to a right critical exercise of the natural reason upon the same Scriptures? It was the absence of any such suggestion in the letters to *The Times*, with one exception, that was the most disturbing feature about them.'[2]

Thus the Liberals of the last generation, like critical scholars

[1] *Theology and Theological Study*, pp. 3-4.
[2] 9th Oct., 1955; printed in *Theology*, Jan. 1956, p. 12. The reference to *The Times* is to the controversy on Fundamentalism in August 1955.

to-day, were asserting the vital theological truth of the human nature of the Bible, which is analogous to that of the true human nature of Christ. They were in fact fighting against the Monophysite heresy which, with its denial of the true humanity of our Lord, is the favourite heresy of orthodox Christians, who in their thought about the Lord whom they worship as the Son of God are always in danger of thinking of Him as a super-human being, omniscient and omnipotent in His human nature, so that His human nature comes to be submerged in the divine, and He is not really seen as true man. Hence the Liberals were in this respect really contending for orthodox Christian theology when they laboured with all their might to show Him as true man and the gospel story as a real human story, and when in their work on the Bible they showed it to be a truly human book, and rescued it from the Monophysite view of it which presented it as a book quite alien from the conditions in which human life is lived to-day. It is indeed true that the Liberals often fell far short of a right view of His Godhead and of the Word of God which the Bible proclaims. But they did lay a much needed emphasis on the other side, on the true humanity.

In doing so they performed a great service to the Church of God, by winning the intellectual respect of the men of their day, and by saving Christianity from being dismissed as an out-of-date superstition which would have to be swept away, much as the old regime in France was swept away by the French Revolution. This they did at the cost of personal suffering; Robertson Smith lost his professorship at Aberdeen, and there were heresy hunts in several countries, America, South Africa and elsewhere; in some parts of the world these still continue to-day.

We who are not Liberals must acknowledge our debt to the Liberals, most of all on this Monophysite issue; and it is relevant in our discussion with conservative evangelicals. R. H. Fuller has lately said in some comments on 'Fundamentalism':[1] 'We have this treasure, the Word of God, in earthen vessels. It is part of the condescension of God that He should have stooped

[1] In the *Religious Book Club Bulletin*, No. 110, Jan. 1956.

to declare His word through the words of fallible men. This is the pattern of divine condescension which runs through the whole of God's self-communication to man—in His Incarnation in the Man Jesus, in His body the Church, in His use of the frail elements of water, bread, and wine in the two sacraments of the Gospel. The Church has constantly been tempted to over-look or deny this wondrous condescension—in Monophysitism which denies our Lord's true human nature, in transubstantia-tion which denies the physical reality of the elements of the bread and wine, in Romanism, with its belief in an infallible Church, and in Fundamentalism which denies the reality of the Bible as a very human book. All the way through, we have to discern the treasure in the earthen vessels: the divinity in Christ's humanity, His Body and Blood in the bread and wine, the Israel of God in that body of fallible and sinful men which we call the Church, the Word of God in the fallible words of men.' Something very important is being said in this quotation, and I shall refer to it again.

But we must return to the Liberals. On the theological side, the original Fundamentalists rightly saw that they were con-fronted with real heresy. Perhaps the central point of all was this: That Religion was being substituted for God. The Develop-ment of Religion was the central point in the interpretation of the Bible that was being presented. The Old Testament was seen as the primary source of materials for reconstructing the evolution of religion in Israel from animism to polytheism, from that to monolatry and from that to Monotheism. The stories in Genesis were ransacked for traces of primitive animism; in the earlier history of Israel in Canaan, Yahweh was worshipped as a tribal god like Chemosh of Moab; from Samuel and David perhaps, He alone was to be worshipped; the belief that He alone exists became definite only in the writing prophets. In their treatment of the New Testament religion was still the governing idea; in the gospels, it was believed that our Lord's teaching, stripped of such irrelevances as the belief in demon-possession and the reality of the miraculous and His belief in His divine nature and mission, provided the religious and ethical pattern which the modern man needed. In the Epistles, we used to hear of Paul's 'Christ-mysticism' as a religious phenomenon.

In all this, the point that was not seen was that this reconstruction of biblical religion was poles apart from the faith which the men of the Bible themselves believed. Scholars could talk of the Exodus-legend; but the Israelites believed that the Lord God had delivered them from Egypt with a mighty hand and an outstretched arm, and that their whole vocation as the People of God depended on the acts of God in history. They feared His judgment. They looked forward to a future divine action, a coming Day of the Lord. The men of the New Testament believed that the Lord God of Israel had visited and redeemed His People. The key-note of the Bible is faith in God.

The account which the Liberals gave of the course of the history was certainly falsified by their misunderstanding of the religion of the Bible. They did not see the relevance to Israel's faith of the Exodus, the Covenant, the sacred Ark; it did not occur to them that it must have been a hard blow to the people's faith when the Ark was lost to the Philistines. The original Fundamentalists were aware of this; rejecting the modern Liberal substitute for the old faith, they rejected with it the reconstruction of the sources of the Pentateuch. J, E, D, and P had in Wellhausen's teaching been correlated with the supposed religious development from animism to monotheism.

But the actual reconstruction of the sources rests on scientific grounds alone. It is perfectly possible to combine a belief that the analysis of the Pentateuch into these sources is mainly correct and that the usual dating of them is roughly right, with such a view of the divine action in the history as has been set forth in this book; many of us have done so for years. But it would not distress us if it were demonstrated that the dating of the documents was all wrong. The modern Scandinavian school think that they have done this; they hold that the various documents did not come one after another in time, but existed side by side with one another in different places. They also think that oral tradition needs to be reckoned with far more than we usually do; Ivan Engnell of Uppsala holds that the works of the prophets and perhaps the other pre-exilic books also went into exile only in the memories of the Israelites, and were first written down in Mesopotamia. All this is a matter of purely scientific theory, and must be proved or disproved on those grounds alone. It does not affect the truth of the faith by which Israel lived, and which is enshrined in the books themselves.

But it is otherwise with the cardinal events of the history. To the old Liberals, with their theory of a development of religious ideas, the Exodus from Egypt seemed irrelevant; hence they were quite happy to talk about the Exodus-legend. It is abundantly clear now that to the faith of Israel the Exodus was vital. Israel believed that the Lord had redeemed them out of Egypt. If there was no historical Exodus, the faith of Israel stood on a basis of mere myth and not of truth. The same is true of the resurrection of our Lord from the dead. To this we must now turn.

We have laid it down as a fundamental principle that scientific inquiry into natural phenomena or history must be free to follow the evidence, and that there can be no honest inquiry if the conclusions which it is to reach are determined before it starts. How then can there be any honest inquiry into the fact of the Resurrection, when we are bound by our faith to confess that our Lord 'suffered under Pontius Pilate, was crucified, dead and buried; the third day He rose again from the dead'?

From a different angle, the difficulty is felt by Rudolf Bultmann, that most radical of critics, who has exercised us all with his plea for the 'de-mythologizing of the Gospel'. He contends 'that the *kerygma* of the New Testament is an attempt to interpret the very earthly history of Jesus of Nazareth by the use of mythological terminology. . . . In speaking of the Resurrection he says, "It would be wrong to raise again at this point the problem of how this preaching arose historically. That would be to tie our faith to the results of historical research. The word of preaching confronts us as the Word of God. It is not for us to question its credentials. It is we who are questioned, we who are asked whether we will believe the word or reject it".[1]

Here Bultmann speaks as a believer, confronted with the Word of God, acutely conscious of the difference between the Word of God and the words of men, and solving the problem by refusing any historical inquiry into the matter and cutting loose from history. Fuller's book is an endeavour to establish the reality of the history through which the Word of God came. But Bultmann has stated a problem which confronts us all. If we believe that our Lord did in fact rise again on the third day, are we dependent on the critical historian for our faith?

St Paul was certainly not prepared to cut loose from history. 'If Christ hath not been raised, your faith is vain; ye are yet in your sins.'[2] The reality of the forgiveness of our sins depends on the truth of the Gospel of God; if Christ did not rise again, that Gospel is not true. Therefore he has begun this fifteenth chapter of I Corinthians with the historical testimony which he has received; and it seems certain that he is quoting here a formula received by him from the apostles at Jerusalem within six or perhaps eight years of the event itself: Christ

died	for our sins	according to the Scriptures	was buried
was raised	on the third day	according to the Scriptures	was seen

by Cephas, by the Twelve, by five hundred brethren, most of whom are still alive when he writes to the Corinthians.

St Paul appeals to history. In his day, as he says, there were many eye-witnesses still alive. We have only the testimony of the written documents, and for the study of these we need the expert help of the critical historian. What he has to do is to interrogate the witnesses. But St Paul needed to do the same; some of his witnesses might have been untrustworthy. Actually, he gives in this passage the certified list of responsible witnesses, as accepted by the Church at Jerusalem. How do we stand?

First, no amount of historical evidence could create faith in our Lord risen from the dead; for faith *in* Him involves a personal self-committal, and this is not at all the same as belief *that*

---

[1] R. H. Fuller, *The Mission and Achievement of Jesus*, S.C.M., 1954, p. 14. Quotation from Bultmann, 'New Testament and Mythology', in *Kerygma and Myth*, edited by Prof. Fuller.

[2] I Cor. 15.17.

He rose again. St James says that the devils believe and tremble; and it is perfectly possible to be intellectually convinced that our Lord rose again and is the Son of God, and still turn away, refuse to repent, refuse to face up to the fact.

Second, if in all matters that concern our faith it is necessary to be honest and resolutely avoid any sort of wishful thinking, it is necessary here above all. One must take account of the historical difficulties, such as the discrepancies between the four evangelists in the account of the visit of the women to the empty tomb, the objections that are made to the story in St Matthew of the guard set at the tomb, the difficulties that arise concerning the nature of our Lord's risen body.

Third, we are able to interrogate our witnesses. Are there any witnesses to testify that at the very beginning there was no belief among the disciples that the Lord was risen, and that this belief first arose after a period of years? No; the evidence is that at the next festival, that of Pentecost, the disciples were at Jerusalem, the place where He had been crucified, proclaiming that He was risen. And who are the witnesses? If there were one narrative only, setting out in a clear and orderly way the movements of the disciples, and the appearances all in order, we might well be suspicious; such an account would no doubt bear all the marks of being an *apologia*, artificially constructed to prove a thesis.[1] Actually we have four accounts, one of which stops short at the Resurrection itself—for the evidence of the manuscripts and the difference of the style make it certain that Mark 16.9–20 is not by St Mark—and the other three give fragmentary records of appearances, all different except that both St Luke and St John tell of an appearance to the disciples in the upper room. When we consider how tremendous and overwhelming such appearances must necessarily have been, we may reflect that these fragmentary accounts are more reliable evidence of the fact than one clear and consistent account could ever be. And what is the character of the evidence that the witnesses give? We may note their reserve and their objectivity; the absence of any effort to produce an effect; that there is nowhere

---

[1] Cf. E. G. Selwyn in *Essays Catholic and Critical*, 1926, p. 295.

any attempt to describe what the Lord looked like, or, again, to describe the emotional feelings of those who saw Him; there are no descriptive epithets. We can say without hesitation that the accounts ring true.

Much more might be said; but this is not the place for a treatise on the Resurrection. But this may be said: that what Bultmann was rightly shrinking from was an attempt, any attempt, to provide a critical proof of the Resurrection. We have attempted no such proof. We have only made some remarks about the character of the narratives as they lie before us, the result of which appears to be to show this: That if the Resurrection is true, it is just such narratives as these that would bear fitting testimony to it.

And if the narratives do in fact stand up to such an interrogation of them, then it remains for each individual to make his response of faith.

VII

The Interpretation of the Bible

IT IS necessary now to make some sort of a review of conservative evangelical opinion on the interpretation of the Bible. I shall use for this purpose chiefly the *New Bible Commentary*, edited by F. Davidson, A. M. Stibbs and E. F. Kevan, and published by I.V.F. in 1953. Needless to say, it is not an official statement of what conservative evangelicals are expected to believe, for there is no such statement; it is a standard work of reference, put out by the I.V.F. I hope that I may be able to praise without damning by faint praise, and to criticize constructively, not like a counsel for the prosecution. I must first gather up what has been said already about Biblical Interpretation and Inerrancy, by putting out a list of questions:

What is the quality of the biblical interpretation given here? Is the effort consistently made to see what was the point of view of each writer and what he was endeavouring to express? Is prophecy treated as the endeavour of the prophet to interpret God's Purpose, or is attention chiefly directed to the literal fulfilment of predictions? Is the scientific duty of honest historical inquiry faithfully carried out, so that the appeal to history is vindicated? Or is the exegesis dominated by some external presupposition, such as that no error of any kind can be admitted in the biblical writings?

Perhaps none of these questions can be answered with a categorical Yes or No; for the general view that is taken is that of a somewhat elastic doctrine of Inerrancy. Thus it is acknowledged that many of the numbers in the Old Testament are unreliable.[1] Also there is some diversity of view; the second of the introductory articles on Inspiration, by Packer, uses the

[1] E.g. on II Chron. 13.17.

rigid word 'infallibility', while the first, by Bromiley, avoids it.

Textual criticism is admitted. On I John 5.7f., the text about the Three Heavenly Witnesses, Leon Morris recognizes that the evidence shows beyond all doubt that this sentence 'was not written by John' and 'does not require attention in any endeavour to understand John's thought'. On Mark 16.9–20, while it is surprising to be told that this is 'one of the major textual problems of the New Testament', the account of the evidence which follows makes it clear that these verses are not by St Mark. On Isa. 62.5, the re-vocalization of the Hebrew text to read 'Builder' in place of 'sons' is accepted. The textual tradition is in fact substantially sound; and as T. C. Hammond says[1] 'the multiplication of readings has not been an unmixed evil' because 'it has awakened the spirit of inquiry' and 'induced a very close study of the sacred text'. Perhaps then more might have been done in this Commentary to notice the really interesting variations of the text which have been occasioned by the exegetical perplexities of the scribes.

As for the exegesis of the text, the effort is consistently made throughout the Commentary to show how the Word of God is spoken through words of men. Here this Commentary compares favourably with other one-volume commentaries in which the main stress is laid on the critical problems in the introductions to the various books, and we have at the end a paragraph beginning 'The religious value of this book is. . . .' In this Commentary we have regularly a good straightforward exegesis, for the help of the reader who wants to study the Bible as the Word of God. In the Old Testament section reference is regularly made to the use of the books in the New Testament.

At the same time the exegesis is on the whole conventional and unenterprising; there is not that penetration into the depths and heights of New Testament theology which we find among our critical 'Biblical Theologians'. To take a pair of instances: Gen. 18.14, 'Is nothing too hard for the Lord' is one of the great texts of the Bible; the word *pala*' which is used here, means 'to

[1] *Inspiration and Authority*, p. 34–5.

be too difficult for', and is used both in the simple form and the derivative *niphla'oth* ('wondrous works', 'marvellous acts') to denote a work of divine salvation in a situation where human resources are at an end. Hence the references given in the R.V. margin to Gen. 18.14 are 'Job. 42.2, Jer. 32.17 and mg., Zech. 8.6, Matt. 19.26, Luke 1.37', truly a splendid list of texts. Yet in this Commentary the point is quite missed, except for a brief mention of it on Matt. 19.26. Again, in the otherwise unsatisfactory commentary on Daniel, much attention is paid to the literal fulfilment of the predictions, but only a few lines on p. 676 to the use of the 'Son of Man' prophecy by our Lord,[1] and the light which it throws on His use of the title; nor is the defect remedied in the commentaries on the gospels. On the Theology of the Old Testament and of the New this commentary is distinctly weak.

It is a serious fault that the exegesis is often trivial and unworthy. We could have looked for real help and genuinely constructive answers on the Old Testament texts which have occasioned popular ridicule, such as the story of Adam and Eve; the question, Where did Cain's wife come from?; the longevity of the patriarchs in the period before the Flood; Lot's wife turned into a pillar of salt; Balaam's ass speaking with a human voice; the sun standing still for a whole day;[2] Jonah's sojourn in the belly of the Fish. In five out of these seven instances the literal actuality of the story is upheld. In another instance, where the sign is given to Hezekiah of the sun going back ten steps (degrees) on the dial of Ahaz,[3] it is explained that this was 'probably due to some refraction of the sun's rays';[4] this is nonsense, and particularly mischievous nonsense in these days when boys and girls at school learn science and know what refraction is.

About the Adam and Eve story, enough has been said in Chapter III. In the Commentary, while the literal meaning is insisted on, the symbolic or theological meaning is indicated. Would it not have been more helpful, in view of the popular

---

[1] Mark 14.62; quoting Daniel 7.13. [2] Josh. 10.12–14.
[3] II Kings 20. 9–11. [4] *New Bible Commentary*, p.320.

difficulty, to lay the whole weight of the exposition on the theological meaning—since it is *this* that is not commonly understood—and to soft-pedal the literal meaning, only making clear that the Fall was a real event?

In the case of 'Sun, stand thou still upon Gibeon',[1] there is this explanation, that in the prose explanation, verse 14, the words 'the sun hasted not to go down' should be rendered 'the sun hasted not to come', i.e. the storm in effect prolonged the darkness. There is here a praiseworthy attempt to meet the popular difficulty (recognized on p. 231), by referring the event, in effect, to God's providence rather than miracle; but unfortunately the proposed rendering seems to be more than dubious. The relation of miracles to God's ordinary providence over His world is the starting-point of the article on Miracles in the *New Bible Handbook*;[2] and could not this have been taken as a guiding-line in the exegesis of these passages? To the modern man, in our scientific age, miracles present a problem; to the biblical writer they did not. The biblical writer, conscious of God's continual presence and action, would therefore naturally and easily express His presence and action by narrating a miracle. We must attend to the *genre* of the story.[3] The things which Balaam's ass in the story says to her master are perfectly true, and the story is inimitably told. We can all delight in it as a story. But when it is insisted that the story must be literally and factually true, is not this to spoil it much as one spoils poetry if one insists on treating it as if it were bald prose? This is not to take the Bible as it is, but to impose on it an alien standard derived from the materialistic thinking of our scientific age. Here, surely, the doctrine of the Inerrancy of Scripture is simply harmful in the exegesis of the text.

I fear the judgment must be that at these points this Commentary is not up to the standard required, most of all for the non-theological reader, in our day.

With regard to the authorship of the books, the doctrine of Inerrancy requires that wherever a book is stated in the text to

[1] Josh. 10. 12.   [2] pp. 75–8.   [3] Cf. p. 44.

be by such-and-such an author, that fixes the authorship. This is to be distinguished from traditional opinions, such as that St Paul wrote Hebrews; the book itself makes no such claim. We may remind ourselves that these problems of authorship belong to the scientific sphere of literary and historical criticism, and the fundamentals of the faith are not involved.

In general this Commentary upholds throughout the principle of Inerrancy in this matter, but not always. Thus whatever words are attributed to Moses in the text were spoken by Moses, but it is not said in the Bible that Moses wrote the Pentateuch. All the commentators on the five books think that he did so. Aalders in his introductory article[1] allows 'conservative scholars' to hold this view, or alternatively a critical theory of his own, that the Pentateuch was compiled in the early days of the monarchy by someone who made use of the extensive Mosaic literature, together with some pre-Mosaic material.[2] The 'documentary theory' is criticized in a not very satisfactory discussion, but is seemingly not tolerated as a permissible theory. But I will not say more about the Pentateuch, as it was discussed in Chapter VI.

With regard to the Book of Isaiah, it is stoutly maintained[3] that the whole book is the work of Isaiah of Jerusalem. Yet it is admitted that chapters 40–66 refer to the period after the fall of Jerusalem, and the otherwise universally accepted view that they were written then is fairly fully stated, with quotations from Peake's commentary, Dean Bradley, C. R. North, G. A. Smith.[4] Yet the conclusion which would ordinarily be drawn from evidence which seems conclusive is not drawn, even though it is admitted that a biblical prophecy ordinarily relates to the situation in which the author himself is speaking. But no: prediction is an element in prophecy, and the Holy Spirit could inspire Isaiah to write words which would not become intelligible till a century and a half later. This consideration, together

---

[1] Ibid., pp. 31–4.   [2] Ibid., p. 34   [3] pp. 558–62.
[4] One point however is missed: that Chaps. 56–66 are usually taken to be a series of detached prophecies, mostly Palestinian and dating from the period down to 450 B.C. This invalidates the use made of the quotation from Angue and Green's *Bible Handbook* on p. 559.

with the universal acceptance of the unity of Isaiah from the time of Ben-sira (about 200 B.C.) onwards, must be held to have decisive weight.[1]

It is true that not all conservative evangelicals hold this view of the unity of Isaiah, and the ordinary view seems to be implied in the passage from p. 1191 which will be referred to a little later. But we must ask, Why is the conclusion which most scholars draw from the evidence not even tolerated? It is a basic principle of scientific study that the conclusions reached should follow from the evidence, and that no external considerations should influence the result. *Some disturbing factor is coming in;* and our real problem is to determine what it is. In this instance, it is not the doctrine of Inerrancy; for the name of Isaiah is nowhere mentioned in the book after chap. 39. What is this disturbing factor?

We get it again in the commentary on Daniel, though here the whole book claims to be by Daniel. There is indeed, in the Commentary, no objection to treating a biblical book as pseudonymous, for it is admitted both here and in the *New Bible Handbook*, p. 201, that Ecclesiastes is not by Solomon; in other words, a biblical book can be inspired and yet not be written by the author whose name it claims. It is argued that the Book of Daniel is by a Daniel who lived in the reigns of Nebuchadnezzar and Darius. (There is a difficulty here, for the Darius known to history did not come to the throne till 522, 75 years after Daniel went into exile as a lad in 597. Perhaps then this Darius is 'some unknown figure'.[2]) On p. 669 there is a really unscrupulous piece of argument, twisting a scientific conclusion in the interests of an apologetic interest: 'It seems most likely that the characteristic of the Aramaic [in which part of Daniel is written] is that which is called "Reich" or "Kingdom" Aramaic, i.e., which was introduced into the Persian Empire by Darius I. Does this fact, however, rule out Daniel as the author? Not at all. It is quite possible that the Aramaic in which Daniel is written is simply a working over or modernizing of the Aramaic in which the book was originally composed.'

[1] Ibid., pp. 558–9, 562.   [2] p. 674.

But some other parts of the Commentary are on a very different level. As I have said, the commentator on Daniel spends much space in working out the detailed temporal fulfilment of the predictions.[1] But in the commentary on the Revelation, Beasley-Murray has an interesting note[2] on the fact that St John was mistaken in thinking that the coming of the Last Things was temporally imminent, and that similarly throughout the Bible prophets are found expecting the coming Deliverance to happen in their own day—in the Old Testament Isaiah, Habbakuk, Jeremiah, Isaiah (chs. 49, 51), Ezekiel, Haggai, Daniel; while in the New Testament St Paul, Hebrews, St James, I Peter, I John, as well as St John in the Revelation all expect the Last Advent of our Lord to happen very soon.

In the New Testament, Bruce's admirable and scholarly article on 'The Fourfold Gospel'[3] admits the whole modern discussion of gospel sources. The commentator on St Matthew, however, with the aid of some dubious exegesis of Matt. 9.9–10 and the parallels,[4] argues that St Matthew is the author. The authorship of St John's gospel is left open,[5] and attention is rightly concentrated on the gospel's theological message. The authorship of Hebrews is left open. The Pastoral Epistles and II Peter are held to be the work of St Paul and St Peter respectively.

There is, of course, no reason why one should not hold a 'conservative' view on any critical problem when, after a full and fair consideration of the whole matter, one holds that the conservative view is right. It was on such critical grounds that E. G. Selwyn, in his Commentary on I Peter,[6] maintained that St Peter was the real author of the Epistle, though Silvanus did the drafting. Or again, many of us feel sure on critical grounds that Ephesians is the work of St Paul, though actually drafted probably by a pupil of his under his supervision, and that in any case it belongs to the same date as Colossians and Philemon. On the other hand, on the same critical grounds many of us feel sure that the Pastoral Epistles are not St Paul's work; that it is not

---

[1] Ibid., pp. 600–1.   [2] p. 1191.
[3] pp. 58–63.   [4] pp. 771, 784.   [5] See on John 21.24.
[6] *The First Epistle of St. Peter*, Macmillan, 1946.

the real Paul who is there speaking to us, but someone else using his name, and, especially in II Timothy, incorporating parts of genuine Pauline letters, as P. N. Harrison seems to have proved. This is not to say that they are 'forgeries', that is to say, writings fraudulently drawn up to present a different teaching from St Paul's. An instance of such forgery would be his allusion in II Thess. 2.2 to an 'epistle as from us' written to the Thessalonians to tell them that the Advent was immediately imminent, and claiming to be from St Paul, if that is the meaning of the words—but it is not certain that it is.

J. C. Fenton, in an article on 'Pseudonymity in the New Testament',[1] in which he shows that 'pseudonymous writing was an accepted literary form in the ancient world; . . . whole books had been put under the name of an ancient figure by the Jews: Enoch, the XII Patriarchs, Moses, David, Solomon, etc. . . . and this practice was continued by the Christians, heretical and orthodox alike'.[2] With regard to the Pastoral Epistles, and II Peter also, 'at a time when the Church was threatened by teachers of new and heretical doctrines, a writer who wished to recall the faithful to the apostolic teaching may have found it necessary to publish his work under the name of an apostle'.[3] In much the same way, most of us hold that Deuteronomy was written by a writer or several writers who in the later period of the monarchy wrote in the name of Moses, because they were writing in the authentic Mosaic tradition and saying for their generation things that they were sure Moses would have said if he had still been with them. And again, the principle of pseudonymity is admitted in this Commentary in the case of Ecclesiastes.

It is strange, then, that A. M. Stibbs should say of the Pastoral Epistles[4] that 'documents which claim to be what they are not cannot carry full weight as canonical Scripture, as the divinely inspired record of apostolic teaching; and therefore, any who

[1] *Theology*, Feb. 1955, p. 54. At one point Fenton is not altogether fair to the I.V.F. Commentary. He gives on p. 53 a table of possibly pseudonymous books in the N.T., and of various modern judgments on them; and here the I.V.F. Commentary does not unambiguously state the first and fourth gospels to be the work of their presumed authors, as we have seen.
[2] Ibid., p. 54.   [3] Ibid.   [4] *New Bible Commentary*, p. 1063.

entertain such doubts about these Epistles had better leave detailed comment on their abiding Christian significance alone', and that 'It will be better for them virtually to leave such documents out of their operative canon of Scripture until they come to a better mind and a saner faith.' Is he not assuming that all pseudonymous writings are 'forgeries' in our sense of the word? and is he not applying a standard of apostolic authorship which would exclude from the canon at least the Epistle to the Hebrews? And here again, the opinion commonly held by conservative evangelicals about the authorship of the Pastorals is not only argued for—which is entirely legitimate—but required, in such a way that other opinions are firmly excluded, and indeed banned.[1]

Before we come to our summing-up, there are two more points that must be raised, with reference to the duty of following scientific inquiry to the conclusions to which it leads, and not twisting it into apologetic.

For a hundred years past, archaeological finds of great importance have been made all over the Middle East, from Egypt to Mesopotamia. Naturally enough, they have provided striking confirmations at many points of the biblical narratives. Thus Professor Albright writes: 'The latest discoveries at Mari on the Middle Euphrates . . . have strikingly confirmed the Israelite traditions according to which their fathers came to Palestine from the region of Harran'.[2] So 'the light cast upon secular history fell incidentally on the Bible also, so that on all sides the cry went up, "Thanks to archaeology, the truth of the Bible has been completely vindicated".'[3] Sir Charles Marston published a book in 1935 on the discoveries made in the previous ten years with the title *The Bible is true*. Parrot continues: 'This well-intentioned though sometimes imprudent enthusiasm at once

---

[1] No more need be said about the case of II Peter, which is regarded as non-authentic by all modern scholars except those who are represented by the I.V.F. Commentary and the *Catholic Commentary*; the same principles apply as in the case of the Pastorals.

[2] From a quotation in André Parrot, *Discovering Buried Worlds*, S.C.M. 1955, p. 110. Parrot was the excavator of Mari.

[3] Ibid., p. 111.

aroused a reaction on the part of sceptics, who asserted just as categorically: "Archaeology, while perhaps confirming certain historical facts, has been unable to do more than that. Above all, it has never proved that in those facts God was really and truly revealing Himself".'[1] And the sceptics were right. *The Bible is true* was a wrong title for a book on archaeology, for it suggested that it was a book not of 'science' but of 'propaganda', written to exploit the discoveries in the interests of ecclesiastical doctrine. Needless to say, any such suggestion defeats its own end; for the strength of the Christian appeal to history depends on complete confidence that the investigations are rigidly scientific and objective. Sir Charles Marston's title was a piece of salesmanship.

Parrot says a little later: 'Although archaeology has confirmed historical facts beyond the shadow of doubt'—and here he illustrates from some tablets found at Babylon listing the rations supplied to certain captives including Ja'uchin king of the land of Jahudu; and this is king Jehoiachin who was deported from Jerusalem in 597 B.C.,[2]—'it would be rash to suppose that it has *always* demonstrated the scrupulous accuracy of *every* historical particular preserved in the Scriptures. A single example: the town of Ai can scarcely have been taken by Joshua (Josh. 7 and 8), for digging has revealed that the city had been destroyed long before the arrival of the Israelites. Its site was indeed a "ruin" (this is precisely what *Ai* means), but it is difficult to believe that the ruin was occupied by a king! Nevertheless a king is mentioned (Josh. 8.1).'[3] This difficulty is recognized in the I.V.F. Commentary: 'The excavation of the site has shown that it was unoccupied between 2000 and 1200 B.C., and lay in ruins all that time (hence presumably its name Ha-ai, "the ruin"). L. H. Vincent has suggested that the inhabitants of Bethel had merely an outpost at Ai of such modest proportions and temporary nature that it has left no remains to betray its existence to the excavator. Such a solution does not tally with the biblical description of it as an inhabited city.' The question is left undecided; but 'it is perhaps safest to accept the possibility that

---

[1] Ibid.   [2] II Kings 24.12–16.   [3] Parrot, p. 113–41.

there was a city there, even though no trace of it has been found in the excavation'.[1]

The second point relates to the Commentary on Genesis 1, the creation-story. It is said here that the account is not 'scientific', in the sense of giving a *modern* scientific account long before its time; had such an account been given, it would have been unintelligible till our own day.[2] But it is suggested that the account may be scientific in its substance; no errors have yet been found (for the 'days' of creation may be interpreted as literal days, or as days of dramatic vision, 'the story being presented to Moses in a series of revelations spread over six days', or as geological ages—'the sun did not exist during the first three days'[3]—and 'while immature science has sometimes . . . charged the record with inaccuracy' . . . 'further scientific research and a deeper study of the inspired record have compelled the withdrawal of such charges, and science has had to acknowledge that what it was only just beginning to discover had all the time been implicit in the biblical statements.'[4]

Yet no reference whatever is given to any scientific books to support these sweeping statements, and it requires only a little reflection to see that this piece of apologetic is nonsense. The commentator ignores altogether the plain fact that the creation-poem presupposes a geocentric universe consisting of a flat earth with a firmament of heaven overhead; see Gen. 1.6–10.

And to a real man of science it would, I imagine, be most irritating to find that some hypothesis which he had thrown out as a possible explanation of some puzzling set of physical facts, was being seized on as if it were a scientific doctrine and used to corroborate the factual accuracy of some phrase or other in the biblical poem. More than this, the whole procedure would, I think, seem to him an outrage on his sense of reverence. He would think of the creation of the universe by Almighty God as a transcendent mystery, not capable of being plumbed by any theories of his own, but lying far beyond and above them; and he would respect the account in Genesis as a mighty poem

[1] *New Bible Commentary*, p. 230.　　[2] Ibid., p. 76.　　[3] Ibid., p. 77.
[4] Ibid., p. 76.

—for such of course it is—setting forth in its own language, not in his scientific language, a transcendent truth.

What are we to say to all this? All through our discussion we have been asking the question *Why?* Why is there all this concern, throughout the Commentary, to maintain at nearly every point the 'conservative' opinion? Forty years ago there was a cogent reason to give: the Liberal critics were teaching heretical doctrine. But that does not hold good now. Is it that a 'conservative' tradition has become established, from which there is an unwillingness to break away? Perhaps; but that cannot be the whole reason. Is it due to fear lest the faith of the simple Christian should be upset by disturbing critical views?

This last point deserves serious attention; but it cannot in any case be the whole reason, for it would imply that the views maintained by the conservative scholars are primarily 'for export'. But that is not the case; they themselves firmly believe the things that they say. It is true, however, that the simple Christian is liable to be bewildered by the things that even orthodox-minded critics say. Much in the Bible seems to be not literally true. He himself is not a scholar or a theologian; where can he find a sure standing-ground?

We are often asked what is the best simple commentary on the Bible. The I.V.F. Commentary sets out to meet the need of the simple Christian, and to a large extent it does so admirably; it might well be recommended as the best simple commentary, if it were not for the serious faults, not least for the non-theological reader, which it has been our duty in this chapter to point out. What then are those faults, from the point of view of the simple Christian? Primarily this: that he is being treated as if he were a child. He is being told that the Bible is literally true, and the critics who deny this are wrong. But this is a dangerous line of defence; for he may at any moment be confronted with a proof that the account of the Creation is unscientific, or have discrepancies pointed out to him. He may have suspected that he was not being told the whole truth about the Bible; having been told that he must believe everything, he may end by believing nothing. This can and does happen.

The true line of defence must surely be this: That in regard to these critical questions the simple Christian should believe and know that there are plenty of Christian scholars who have faced out all the critical difficulties, and still hold to the Faith and preach the Christian Gospel of salvation. After all, the Christian scholar holds an important place in the economy of the Church. He deserves to be trusted and he will be trusted, when he does his duty honestly, and inspires confidence as a man who is not a mere apologist, but a lover of truth.

But the simple Christian needs also to know and understand for himself the facts about his Bible. Much may be done to help him in sermons; but there is need of more discussions of the things that are said in sermons, more adult education, more reading. The simple Christian needs to know for himself what is genuine Christian teaching, and what is not. Every day he is hearing things said, reading things in the newspapers or in novels, seeing things on the films, which are contrary to the Faith; and he ought to be in a position to say for himself what the Christian answer is. He needs help in all this; but he is not a child, and it is for him to tackle his problems and find his way through them.

To the question asked on the previous page, I think the real answer is this. We live in a scientific age, and hence imbibe a materialistic notion of what Truth is. Truth seems to us to be first of all the truth of material fact, such as that which science studies. It is for this reason that it seems so plausible to think that if the Bible is true, it must be literally and factually true. And here, surely, is the root of the answer to the questions which the I.V.F. Commentary poses to us. We have had instance after instance of this materialistic notion of Truth, down to the last instance of all, the relation of the creation-story in Genesis to scientific fact.

Let me illustrate. I have had students who protested that the Transfiguration of our Lord could not be a 'vision', though the gospel so describes it.[1] They wanted an 'objective' Transfiguration, and (since to their minds the real was the material) it must have been visible to any chance passer-by. Yet only three chosen disciples were permitted to see the Transfiguration; it may be that at that time only they were capable of seeing it and seeing it truly. For to see it truly was to grasp the spiritual reality mediated by the visible sight. Or, to take a very easy instance: when St Paul says that at the Last Day 'the trumpet shall sound', does he mean a 'real' trumpet made of brass? No one will say this. There is such a thing as spiritual reality, which to our human minds can only be expressed in symbolic language, by means of imagery, by poetry, by music.

Michael Roberts showed in his book *The Modern Mind* that this materialistic point of view is relatively recent; it derives from Aristotle, mediated through the thought of the scholastics, and received a strong impulse from the early physicists, and passed, through Hobbes, into the rationalistic philosophy of the following period.[2] But the middle ages were to a large extent innocent of it, and the Bible is innocent of it altogether, for it freely speaks of spiritual reality in symbolic terms.

This is why the *New Bible Handbook* was right in saying that in the Fall-story it is impossible to draw the line between the literal and the symbolic, and in noting at this point the parallel with the Last Things, which can only be described in symbolic terms and by means of imagery. It is impossible to present a rationalized and coherent account of the resurrection-body. We can only speak, incoherently, of a body that is the same and yet different, real but not material. For this, there is a really suggestive analogy in the little creature swimming about in a pond, which is later to go into the chrysalis- or nymph-stage and emerge as a dragon-fly, adapted to the conditions of life in the air above.[3] But the world of the creature in the pond is bounded by the level surface of the water, and to it, if it could think and speak, the conditions of life in the air above would be completely incomprehensible, incapable of being expressed

[1] Matt. 17.9.
[2] See, for this, my book *The Authority of the Old Testament*, pp. 93–100.
[3] Cf. the *Encyclopaedia Britannica*, art. 'Dragon-fly'.

in its thought or language. Such, for us, is 'spiritual' reality. We can apprehend heavenly things only 'through a glass darkly'[1]—that is, like a reflection in the metal mirrors polished by hand which were in use in St Paul's day.

This is why it is wrong to demand that everything in the Bible shall be 'true' in the modern materialistic sense. And does this give the key to the problems which the I.V.F. Commentary raises? Is it unconsciously dominated by the materialistic, intellectualistic view of truth which comes so readily to us in a scientific age? Is this the reason why medical students and science students take so readily to what is called Fundamental-ism—that their minds are specially conditioned by their scienti-fic studies? And is this the reason why the Book of Daniel has got to be written by a man called Daniel, because otherwise the statements in that book would be literally untrue? Is it that a style of thinking which is alien to the Bible is being imposed forcibly upon it? And is this the reason why the man in the street thinks that if Balaam's ass did not speak, the Bible is not true?

Yet the Bible itself is the supreme witness to the reality of a truth that is true but is not capable of being fully expressed in our materialistic human language.

[1] I Cor. 13.12.

VIII

The Religion of Experience

OUR discussion of the Interpretation of the Bible and the Truth of the Bible, which has occupied five chapters, has not been a merely academic disputation. It has a direct relevance to the manner in which the Gospel is proclaimed in the world. So it is that conservative evangelicals always see it; the Word of God which is heard in the Scriptures is to be preached to men and received by faith for the salvation of souls. The scholarly minded among them are watching over the Word of God in the Bible, lest it be misapprehended and treated as the mere word of men. Many others have their attention so fixed on the Word of God that they are simply not interested in critical studies; such was the great C. T. Studd, one of the Cambridge Seven who went to China in 1885. But it has been one of the chief aims of this book to show that critical studies cannot be thus left on one side. In these last three chapters we must see that similar problems arise in the preaching of the Gospel in the world and the life of the Church.

C. T. Studd was a great evangelical, a heroic figure, one of the saints, in many ways like St Francis of Assisi, and like him not at all interested in intellectual problems. As a young man, he was a cricketer of the very first rank, captain of the Cambridge XI in 1883, as were two of his brothers in 1882 and 1884. The three of them were in the Cambridge XI which defeated the Australians in 1882, and C. T. played in the famous Test Match at the Oval on 29th August, when the Australians won by eight runs, and he went that autumn to Australia with the team which recovered the Ashes. In the following year he left cricket and left all to serve the Lord in China, in that very distinguished team of seven men which finally sailed in February

1885, to dress as Chinamen and live in all things with the Chinese. C. T. gave away all his money, and made as complete a surrender of himself as was humanly possible, desiring to be obedient in all things to the Lord's will and trust Him for everything. The age of miracles began again, though never paraded or advertized as such; several times, in extreme sickness, he and his friends used the apostolic anointing with oil, even if the only oil available were kerosene, and were healed. He married in China—it was a unique courtship—and after ten years felt it to be his duty to return home. From 1900 to 1906 he was in India, from 1910 onwards in Africa; in the intervals he was in Britain and America, where he had a part in the founding of the Student Volunteers and the S.C.M. He went to Africa at the age of fifty-two, against all medical and other advice, and penetrated from Egypt to the Belgian Congo by cycle and on foot. There he lived till 1931, in the heart of Africa, doing an altogether pioneer missionary work; meanwhile his wife at home was organizing support for the mission, and by 1923 there were forty European workers there.[1]

An Anglican friend writes thus to me from England: 'What strikes us all so much, I suppose, about the whole astonishing record of Protestant (i.e. mainly 'Fundamentalist') missionary enterprise is its staggering childlike faith and love, with its great key-notes "Nothing too precious for Jesus", "All one in Christ Jesus", and so on, and the sense of utter dependence on the Father and clear guidance of the Holy Spirit; on all of which God has set His seal over and over again, deliberately choosing "Fundies" as you might say, when one feels He might just as easily have chosen "Catholics" for some of His most heroic and delicate and arduous labours.'

Then there has been Dr Billy Graham's preaching. Here is part of one of the letters from *The Times* correspondence (22nd Aug. 1955): 'I am a university graduate, and a comparatively successful business man of thirty-one. I lived with no Church, Bible, or other religious background until last year, and in spite

---

[1] *C. T. Studd, Cricketer and Pioneer,* by Norman P. Grubb, London, Religious Tract Society, 1933.

of having many friends, good health, worldly goods, and no particular worries, I was frustrated, dissatisfied, and unhappy with life. I wanted, somewhere inside me, to be good and to do good, but somehow always failed to come up to even my own standards. At Harringay on 3rd May 1954 I heard the New Testament gospel for the first time in my life. Since then my life has been completely changed—pride, snobbery, frustration, anxiety, and a meaningless existence have been replaced by love, joy, and an abundant and purposeful life. What I could not do, Christ has done. This is supernatural; this is not in the realm of "modern scholarship", or the reason of man—this is a pragmatic, living experience of God.' Reading through that correspondence, one longs that many of the critics of Fundamentalism might know what the Fundamentalists have known.

But there is another side to it. Conversion is a beginning; but after it there is a whole new life to be lived, from youth to old age; a life within the believing and worshipping church-community. There are difficulties to be met, problems to be solved, both by the individual in his personal life, and in the common life of the Christian fellowship.

It can and does happen that newly-converted young people go about saying that their parents are no better than pagans— I heard this lately from one converted by the Evangelical Union, and I heard it once from an Anglo-Catholic—and it is not right. And again, they think in the glow and enthusiasm of their new-found faith that they will be able to live perfect lives, without any sin, and will always keep the joy that they knew in their conversion.

Here they do not always get right advice. The Adelaide *Advertiser* has for some months been publishing 'Answers to Questions' by Dr Billy Graham; generally wise and good, but sometimes dangerously misleading, as in the reply to the following question: 'Six months ago I responded to your call, and came forward and gave my life to Christ. The joy I felt then has all left me. How can I find it again?' The answer was: 'We can't always stay on the mountain-peaks of faith. Sometimes every

Christian goes down into the valley. But there are new heights to climb. You can recapture the glow which you felt when you first gave your heart to Christ if you would know the joy which comes to those who walk with the Master: (1) Read the Bible every day. Don't let this become an empty form. Read to find God's message for you. Think about what you've read, and ask God to interpret His message to you. (2) Pray, not once but many times a day. Pray for others as well as yourself. (3) Take an active part in the work of your church. Working together we can accomplish great things for Christ, and we keep our lamps of faith bright as we rub shoulders with other Christians. (4) Witness for Christ. Every day tell at least one person what Jesus has done for you.

'Do these four things: Read the Bible. Pray. Work. Witness. Then you'll experience again the joy you felt when you first gave your heart to Christ.'[1]

The four things are all good things to do. But is it good advice, to lay the emphasis on recapturing the glow and not on glorifying God? and to seek to gain this end by a series of 'works', of activities of one's own? Would not the right advice be: (1) to examine himself whether he did wholly give his life to God, or was he keeping something back? and (2) having dealt with this, to cease to worry about his feelings, and go forward, in faith and with thanksgiving?

There are some urgent personal problems here. I propose to deal with them, by presenting a 'digest' of part of a Swedish novel, *Stengrunden*, which ran into its seventh edition within eight months, but has never been translated into English.[2] The author is Bo Giertz, who after about eighteen years of parochial ministry, became in 1949 Bishop of Gothenburg. The story depicts the situation in Sweden about 1879, when the country was full of revivalist movements. The answer can be given far better in the dramatic form of his narrative than in a homiletic discourse of my own. I will let the story speak for itself. It is a tale of a Swedish parish, for which he has invented the name

---

[1] The Adelaide *Advertiser*, 26th Jan. 1956.
[2] *Stengrunden* means 'Stony Ground'—the stony ground of the human heart.

Ödesjö, and of three young priests (the word *präst* is in regular use in the Scandinavian Lutheran Churches) who went to it at three different dates: (i) about 1809, when the young man, imbued with the eighteenth-century Deism, came across the old evangelical faith alive in the peasant people, (ii) about 1879, and (iii) 1934–40, the contemporary scene.

It is the second part of the novel that is here given in condensed form. The young priest is himself imbued with the revivalist ideas; to the 'true believers' the established Church of Sweden seemed dry, cold and formalistic. To partake of the Sacrament in the church seemed to them to be 'eating with the swine'; could not they have a real communion-service in which only Believers should take part? Such a service was held about 1875 in the *Missionshus* at Uppsala, and our young pastor is imagined as having taken part in it.[1] I need not say that I have the author's full and cordial consent to make this use of his work. He has, however, asked me to point out clearly that a short 'digest' such as I have made cannot do justice to the niceties of character-drawing in his story, but can only show the main lines of it in its theological bearings. He has also made a few corrections of my text.

JESUS ONLY

(i) *Three days before Christmas*

The Rector of Ödesjö is a man who loves God and loves his people, genial, intelligent, and well-read; but he is getting on in years, and suffers from rheumatism, so that he is no longer able to do much parish visiting. He has therefore applied to the Chapter of Linköping diocese for an assistant priest. It is three days before Christmas, and bitterly cold; but there has been little snow. The new clergyman arrives, Pastor Fridfeldt; he turns out to be a young man who has been deeply influenced by the Revival.

They talk together; he is told about the parish, and they chat

[1] See p. 109 below.

awhile about the Revival. Then the old Rector breaks off, and goes on to reminiscences of old soldiering days, called out by the pictures on the walls; he also has something to drink with his dinner. All this is a little shocking to Fridfeldt, and he feels that he must make his position clear. 'My Rector must know from the start that I am a Believer.' – 'That is good to hear, but what do you believe *in*?' – 'But surely, Rector, you know what a Believer is?' – 'There can be various sorts of believers, my son; I am only asking, what *you* believe in.' – 'In Jesus, of course; I mean, I have given Him my heart.' – 'Is that something worth giving to the Lord?' – 'But . . . but—if you do not give Jesus your heart, how can you be saved?' – 'Right indeed, my son! But it is no less true that if you think you are saved because you have given Jesus your heart, you are not saved. Do you see—it is one thing to choose Jesus to be your Lord and Saviour, to give Him your heart and make your decision for Him; and to think how glad He must be to reckon you as one of His little flock. And it is quite another thing to believe in Him as the Redeemer of sinners, "of whom I am chief". One does not choose for oneself a Redeemer who has made atonement for one's sin, nor give Him one's heart. What is that "heart", after all, but a rusty old tinpot on a rubbish-heap—scarcely a fit thing for a birthday-present! But then comes our wonderful Lord, walking past, and takes pity on the wretched tinpot, and with His walking-stick lifts it out of the dirt and takes it home with Him.' Fridfeldt thought it was really most irreverent to talk in this way; but the old man went on, 'Do you see, there are two different ways of believing, almost like two different religions. And yet there is a way from the worse to the better; first a person believes in Repentance, and then comes to believe in God's Grace. And I think you are started on the way.'

The Rector then closed this conversation, and proceeded to give instructions for a series of visits to be made in the course of the next two or three weeks; there were Christmas parcels to be taken to some houses, and a spiritual ministry to be carried out in each of them. All this was specified in detail, in a manner which showed an intimate knowledge of the life that was being lived in those homes.

(ii) *Spring-time*

It was now March, and there was spring in the air. The after-meeting at the mission-house was over, and the people were singing hymns as they walked home under the stars. Among them was Churchwarden Ollson; he was treading on the clouds, full of a holy devotion and a heavenly joy. His heart was wholly at peace; all his prayers, his desires and longings had come true. Now they had an assistant-priest who was a Believer; the people had discerned this at once in his preaching at Christmas. His sermons won their hearts; they were popular in style, full of illustrations, and easy to follow and to remember. There had been several conversions; the Spirit had been manifestly at work; threatened divisions within their circle had all melted away.

Fridfeldt was walking with him. He too had been quite overwhelmed by the events of the last three months: to think that he should thus have fallen at once into his place, and have become an instrument of the Revival, among a people so spiritually mature and so responsive! This evening he had been preaching on the Prodigal Son and the Father's love, and the presence of the Spirit had been manifest when one after another had prayed at the after-meeting and thanked God that at last they had come home to their Father's house.

But there was something else to do that night. The church-warden was taking him back to his own house, to talk, with his cousin Eric, of a sad scandal which had arisen among the Believers. It was this. Daniel, one of their pillars, and the richest man in the village, had been approached by Karl-August, a small tenant-farmer and a poor man, on Monday last to buy some hay to feed one of his cows; for there had been a poor hay-harvest in the previous year. Daniel said that he had absolutely none to spare. Karl had begged and pleaded, but in vain; he had said that he would have to slaughter the cow, but again was refused any hay. Then he had no option but to sell the cow, and Daniel got it at a cheap price. Next day the cow fell sick, and Daniel had to kill it; it had evidently drunk something harmful. Now Daniel was going about saying that Karl-August had cheated him.

It was a dreadful thing that this should happen among the Believers; and the three of them discussed the matter in all its aspects. Nor was it an isolated instance; there had been incidents like this before. In the end they all went round to see Karl-August, and gained the impression that he was the innocent party. While they were there, Daniel arrived in his buggy; he had come to demand from Karl-August the return of the money that he had received for the cow. The Pastor challenged him and denounced him; he refused to accept any rebuke, and drove away in a rage.

So the matter came to the Rector, and at nine next morning he arrived at the hamlet in his buggy, to find something like a riot beginning. Daniel was preparing to take away half of the cow for sale, the whole population was assembled, and a young man, Johan Jonnson, was leading the protest with oaths and curses, and had just struck Daniel a blow on the face.

As the Rector drove up, all the tumult was suddenly hushed. He went into the house, posting Fridfeldt at the door, and he saw Johan first. 'Johan, how can a Christian man behave as you have just been doing?' There was no answer. (Fridfeldt thought to himself, I should never have said that; I should have made it clear to him that he is not a Christian at all.) 'What do you think God thought of it, when He heard you cursing? I think He thought, This lad has been baptized, he is one of My children, but he has not been glorifying Me to-day. And will this hand of mine have to witness against you at the Judgment day? Let this hand bear witness that it has held out to you the Holy Sacrament, and you received it into your mouth. Yet that same mouth has this day been uttering curses. Should a Christian man so behave?' At last a reply: 'No, Rector.' – 'I knew that, Johan; now you say the same. And now, I will not draw this hand back, till it can witness for you and not against you. Will you promise me two things? First, every evening to pray God to forgive you your sins and help you to be a better Christian.' – 'But what if I forget sometimes?' – 'Then you pray the same prayer the next morning. Agreed?' – 'Yes, Rector.' – 'The second is: Will you promise to see Daniel as soon as I have finished speaking with him, and tell him that you have behaved like a fool, and desire the matter to be forgiven and forgotten?' – 'I promise it, Rector.'

Then Karl-August was called in. (Fridfeldt thought, If he treats the ungodly as Christians, how will he deal with the Believers?) 'Now I want you to answer me a question: Karl-August, did you know that the cow was sick when you sold it to Daniel? But no, before you answer, first read out from this Bible —the place is found—Revelation, chapter 21 verse 8.' He read: 'But the fearful, and unbelieving and the abominable, and murderers, and whoremongers, and sorcerers, and all liars, shall have their part in the lake which burneth with fire and brimstone; which is the second death.' – 'Now, did you know that that cow was sick?' The answer came in a whisper: 'Yes, Rector.' – 'Thanks be to God. Now there is hope for your soul. What will you do next?' – 'Ask God to forgive me.' – 'And then?' – 'Give the money back.' – 'Good: and then? But I see I must help you. Ask Daniel to forgive you.' Karl-August shivered in his whole body as he said 'Ye-es'. – 'God bless you, Karl-August, for now the angels in heaven are rejoicing that a little brother has come home. Now go and get the money.'

Daniel came in next, looking pale and sullen. He had washed the blood off his face. To him the Rector said, 'Daniel, you have been shamefully deceived, but it is all going to be made good. Karl-August has gone to fetch the money, to restore it to you.' The man's countenance brightened visibly. 'Also he is coming to offer you his hand and ask you to forgive him. Will you accept his hand, receive the money, and let bygones be bygones?' – 'Most gladly', said Daniel. He had never expected this.

'That is well', said the Rector. 'But there is another person too, by whom you have been shamefully deceived; and this is much more serious. You see, Daniel, on Monday last there was a conversation in heaven, like that in the Book of Job. The Lord

God said, The Accuser has had so much to say lately about one of My servants down below at Ödesjö, that I think of putting him to the test, to see whether all the tales are true about his meanness and his desire to have a well-filled note-case and many fat cows. And so God sent to you a poor tenant-farmer who wanted to buy some hay. And God said to His angels, Now we shall see whether My servant is upright and faithful and will let him have the hay cheap. But the Accuser also went on his way, and got there in time, and whispered to him, Daniel, don't behave like a fool. If the fodder cannot be bought, he will have to sell the cow, and it is not every day that you can buy so good a cow so cheap. And now there was great excitement in heaven, to see whether Daniel would allow himself to be deceived by his worst enemy. Now, Daniel, how did it go? Were you deceived?' Daniel would not reply. – 'Daniel, the heavenly Father is looking at you now. On Monday last He was much grieved on your account; shall it be so again? Answer me: were you deceived by Satan last Monday?' – 'Yes, Rector, I was.' – 'God be praised for that answer, Daniel; it is the strongest witness to Him that you have given for a long time. And now let us see if we cannot put this matter to rights. You have failed to help your neighbour. Would it not be best if we tried to help him now?' – 'How do you mean, Rector?' – 'I mean that he is a poor man, and the loss of his cow is a heavy blow to him. Will you reckon up what is the value of the half of the carcase that you were intending to sell to-day, and also what the cost of another good cow would be? Then we can tell how much needs to be made up.'

A new cow would cost from 55 to 65 *riksdaler*; half the carcase was worth 15, the whole was worth 30. The Rector proposed a collection; he put down 5 *riksdaler* himself, and Daniel put down 10; the rest was soon collected in the village. Before he drove away, the Rector gave them a brief talk on 'Ye are the body of Christ, and severally members thereof.'

On the way down, churchwarden Ollson was full of reminiscences; here a driver and a team of oxen, who had perished in a snow-storm, had been dug out; here there had once been a private distillery, which had been a cause of scandalous drunkenness, and which in his earlier days the Rector had uprooted, together with other similar establishments, not without danger to his life. Fridfeldt, to whom this had been a day of wonders, was amazed to hear this; had his Rector been a champion of temperance? 'Did my Rector do all this?' he said. 'Why do you never talk about it? This is something that the separatists ought to think over.' – 'One ought not to talk about oneself, for then one prevents them from seeing Jesus', said the Rector; and Fridfeldt saw that it implied a rebuke to himself, for he himself constantly talked in his sermons about himself and his spiritual experiences.

He had learnt very much that day. But he had more to learn yet.

(iii) *The Feast of the Transfiguration*

It was a perfect summer's day; a Sunday in August, and the Feast of the Transfiguration. Fridfeldt was to preach; but he himself was in a state of the greatest disquiet.

A letter had come last night from Conrad, an old friend from school and college days, and now a schoolmaster at Örebro. At Uppsala they had gone through the experiences of the Revival together, and had together given their hearts to God there, and had taken part in the great communion-service in the Uppsala Mission-house for Believers only, four years before. The letter said:

> Dear Brother of my heart in the Lord,
> God's peace be with you.
> You are the first to whom I am writing, on this the greatest day of my life! I cannot tell you how happy I am! Now for the first time I realize that I have become a real Christian. I have been baptized! Really baptized with the true baptism, according to our Lord's will and the witness of Scripture. What a liberation! There are no words to describe it. It has been a hard battle, but now victory has come. To God be the glory!

. Since I came here I had been more and more unhappy. I found that I was not in fact what I had for so long thought myself to be, a real Christian. I had no power to control my evil thoughts; I was tormented with pride, and the storms of impure desires all but overwhelmed me. I cannot describe the misery of it. I tried all sorts of remedies. I prayed much, and that helped for a time; but the foul imaginations came back. I read the Word of God often; but even whilst I read, the impure thoughts returned, and I cannot describe the vileness of them.

Then by God's providence I met with some real Christians at the Mission-house here, and told them of my plight. They opened my eyes, and showed me that I could not expect to gain the victory over sin so long as I did not obtain the gift of the Holy Spirit through a real baptism. We looked in the Scriptures and there it was; nothing about infant baptism, and baptism must be preceded by faith and repentance. It was a hard thing to have to face, especially for me, with my Degree in Philosophy; was I to act as if I were an infant, and go down into the font? I should never have done it, if I had not been so hard pressed with sins, and seen that there was no other hope for me of joy and peace.

And now it has happened! The days that have followed have been the happiest of my life. I have entered on the new life and experienced its power. The storms of temptation have passed quite away; I am filled with a glad peace, I walk in a light such as I had never seen before. Oh, that all who are unhappy might see and know how good a thing it is to commit oneself wholly to the Lord, and follow the way of obedience right to the end!

Fridfeldt read the letter again. 'The way of obedience right to the end.' Was this God's way for him also? Point by point, his own experience had been the same. After the great crisis in March, he had after a while dropped back to the old level. Also the Revival in the parish had stagnated; many had dropped away, and the fervour of the meetings had declined. Had that fervour been the physical effect of under-nourishment and en-feebled bodies, while the fruits and crops of the new year were not yet ready? He had not suggested this to anyone else; but he was deeply disappointed. He felt that the people also were doubting the reality of their experience. The one person who seemed to show real signs of God's grace was young Johan Jonnson, and he had never been properly converted.

He asked himself whether it was his fault. He had not been God's instrument as he should have been. He had indeed set himself to crucify the body of sin, but it had been a dying without any resurrection to new life. For three weeks after the crisis all had been well. Then there had been a chilly and rainy April morning when he had lain in bed late, and had come to break-fast without saying his prayers. The Rector had chatted about old school days; and all day after that the thoughts of the un-godly world had dominated his mind. He had tried to pray, but felt an intense distaste for prayer, and soon gave up. He had not overcome this distaste till late in the afternoon, when he had pulled himself together half an hour before he was due to go to a prayer-meeting; and on the way thither he had thought to him-self that he had now prayed chiefly in order that he might acquit himself well at the prayer-meeting, and save his reputation.

He had worked away at the garden of his soul, till his fingers bled. Why had he borne so little fruit for God? He had burnt all his coloured neckerchiefs when he had found himself picking the best among them. He had given up drinking coffee, because he found he was so fond of it. All this had brought him no peace of mind.

Had he received God's word for him that very day—'the way of obedience right to the end'? He knew that he did not set much store by infant baptism; for him, it was conversion that meant everything. That real conversion might demand another bap-tism was a new idea to him; yet it was plain how important a thing baptism was in the New Testament. But it was a hard way. He would have to give up his priesthood. Was this then a fetter that he must break? To become a free preacher, serving the great Revival—what a great thing it would be to renounce all and go out, free, poor, burning with apostolic zeal! If only he could find peace with God, he would gladly follow the way of obedience right to the end.

For a moment a doubt arose: what if the peace of which Conrad had written were to prove to be only a passing phase? What if it in turn were to pass away after a few weeks? He put aside the doubt: it *could* not be so! If so, there would be no way left to find peace. Was it not a call from God that Conrad's letter had brought? In any case he must make a decision that very day, for he had half-promised to attend a meeting that afternoon at which this question was to be discussed. He knelt down, that Sunday morning in the rectory garden, and prayed God earnestly to guide him in the right way, and show him a clear sign.

Then, suddenly, he heard his name called. A sick visit. Frans at Sjöstugan was dying; there had been a heart attack. He must go at once. Frans had been a grenadier; he was old now, but he had been a godly man, and during a previous visit he had talked quietly and maturely about spiritual things. All would surely be well at the death-bed.

When he came to the house, there was little that he could do. The dying man was unconscious, but from time to time he uttered words. First he seemed to be back in his military days; then there came a full-blooded oath. What had happened to his godliness? thought Fridfeldt. Then he complained that he had been cheated over a calf. Then he began to speak of religious things: 'She does not pray as much as I do.' Fridfeldt thought how like this was to his own case. What if it were he that now lay dying? what if bits out of his past, and of his lustful imaginations, were to come out in this way? What would people think? His conscience smote him: did not he think only of his own good reputation? Was not all his Christianity a mere mockery, and he himself as full of sin as that dying man? The only difference was that he was fully conscious and in control of himself, and that he, out of respect for his good name, kept a strict rein on his utterances, so as to conceal the uncleanness within. But to God all hearts were open.

Soon, some neighbours came to help in the house. He looked at his watch; it was almost half past nine, and he must be at church at ten, ready to take the service and to preach. And his sermon was not prepared.

He hurried down to the church. There was only one thing that he could do: pick up a printed sermon and preach it. He found in his room a sermon on the Transfiguration by the great preacher Schartau, which the Rector had lent to him; he would preach that.

So it was that fifty-five years after his death a great man of God preached again in Ödesjö church a sermon which he had once given in Lund Cathedral; he preached to the people assembled there, but above all and especially to the man standing in the pulpit.

The title of the sermon was 'Jesus only'. 'When they [the three disciples] had lifted up their eyes, they saw no man, save Jesus only', Matt. 17.8. 'So it is that when the sinner's spiritual eyes are first opened, he looks down, and he sees his own unsaved and lost condition. . . . The soul looks in on itself, and sees its own corruption side by side with God's holiness and its guilt with God's righteousness.' (This is all about me, thought Fridfeldt.) 'But then the Holy Spirit lifts up his spiritual eyes to Jesus only. . . . It is a blessed thing when the faithful soul in its prayer lifts up its eyes and fixes them on Jesus, not looking *around* on its own wandering thoughts, nor *behind* itself at Satan who tries to make out that its prayer is all in vain, nor *within* at its own sluggishness and feeble devotion, but *upwards* at Jesus who sits at God's right hand and pleads for us.'

So the sermon went on. To lead the soul to Jesus only is the aim of all spiritual awakening. Jesus only is the ground of our justification and salvation; for He died upon the cross for our sins, bearing our sins and making atonement. 'So God in His mercy does not look on our good deeds: He looks on His dear Son, not on our good deeds, for then He would have to look on our evil deeds which are mixed in with the good.' (This is the answer, thought the preacher: sin continually present, and continually being forgiven. There is hope, then, for Frans at Sjöstugan. And he seemed to see a great Cross up in the sky, with its arms stretched out over the whole countryside: a redeeming, atoning, all-pitying Love, for all those evil hearts among which sin was active like snakes in a viper's den. Jesus only!)

And finally, Jesus only is the ground of the new life. 'Only faith in Jesus, only the clinging of the hungry soul to Him, brings light into the soul, so that the Sun of Righteousness may arise within it, and God may dwell there. . . . Then the mind of Jesus becomes the soul's mind, His will becomes its will; so that it *always* desires to be and *sometimes* is able to be humble like Jesus, patient like Jesus, obedient like Jesus, pure in heart like Jesus.'

That afternoon Fridfeldt went to the meeting. It was a long meeting, and he spoke a good deal. At the end of the meeting someone said, 'This afternoon the Pastor has given us a sermon all his own, which we shall not soon forget. Now I feel fully sure of my original baptism, and I need no other.' The chief points that were discussed were these:

First, a woman made the dogmatic assertion that a real Christian is one who has a clean heart. The meeting questioned whether this was true. Could she, the speaker, say that she herself had a clean heart? How long had she been converted? Fifteen years. Had she had a clean heart all that time? Fridfeldt summed it up by saying that the foundation and ground of the state of grace is not our hearts, clean or unclean, but the righteousness of Jesus and His merits. God saves sinners.

Then came a question whether the Atonement, the Reconciliation of man with God, is something that has happened outside us and without us: is it not something that has its effect within us? Fridfeldt replied to this, quoting Romans 3.23–6, and affirming that the Reconciliation has first taken place outside us, in Christ's own saving death. If it happened altogether within us, 'that would mean that we are Christians and can stand before God in virtue of a change in our hearts. Friends, can any of us say that his heart has been so changed that he can stand before God on this ground?'

Finally, there was Fridfeldt's own problem, posed in Conrad's letter. This was how the matter now appeared to him: 'If I had decided to be baptized again, that would have been an endeavour to propitiate God with yet another work of my own, and climb up to heaven following a way that seemed to be the way of obedience. But already I had tried everything. I had sought to deny to myself all sorts of worldly things, clothes, food, drink, anything in which I found that I took delight. I was tempted by the idea of a second baptism, because that seemed to be one final offering of obedience. Now I see that this was a temptation, to seek to escape God's wrath and be justified by an act of my own—*my* obedience. Now I see that the sacrifice which is pleasing to God is a broken and contrite heart which sees its own corruption and sin and takes refuge in Jesus only. To have been baptized over again would have been an act of unbelief in God, not of faith in what He has done for me.'

As he walked home in the summer evening, he passed the old church, and felt a great love for it. The Church is our mother, for she has given us the Baptism by which we became Christians. The old Rector was right when he dealt with his parishioners as God's children, and so quite naturally imposed on them the demands of Christian duty. And in the church, which had stood there for so many generations, the work of God had been going on long before he was born. How good it was to enter on such an inheritance! How great a thing it was to be a priest!

That evening at supper, he said to Fru Hollemann, their housekeeper, that he wished to have some coffee. (The Rector did not drink coffee at night, and was smoking his pipe instead.) Fru Hollemann felt this as a small triumph, for she had always said that it was no sin to drink coffee. Fridfeldt replied, 'What the Law of God forbids is all wrong desire, and all selfishness in thought, word and deed. If I were setting up to myself the ideal of living a perfect and sinless life, I should not dare to drink coffee, or even to go on with this conversation now. But there is a better way: "the life which I now live in the flesh, I live by the faith of the Son of God, who loved me and gave himself for me." Therefore I think that I can well take to drinking coffee again. And perhaps a day will come when after the pattern of my Saviour I may dare to go out and sit down among sinners and drink with them a glass of wine.'

'Fie', said Fru Hollemann, 'now the Pastor is beginning to talk just like the Rector!'

'I can desire nothing better', said Fridfeldt quietly.

There was still another visit to pay that night, to old Frans at Sjöstugan.

IX

The Ground of Unity

WE HAD in the last chapter a Swedish churchman's view of the historic Church and of the 'Believers' who thought that the Church, being a mixed body with many unworthy members, could not be the true Church of God; those who had given their lives to Christ were 'real Christians', and having been delivered by Him from the guilt and power of sin, were now enabled to live sinless lives. But we were shown in the narrative how the 'real Christians' nevertheless did sin; there were scandals occurring among them, and they were seeking after justification by works, in their effort to live holy lives. The conclusion was that the old Church, with the acknowledged sinfulness of its members, witnesses to the pure unmerited grace of God by the word of the forgiveness of sins preached from its pulpit, and by the sacraments which it administers.

But let us turn to see what St Paul says. The address of the First Epistle to the Corinthians is to 'the Church of God which is at Corinth', though he well knows how many sins among its members he will rebuke in the course of the Epistle. The first of these, in chaps. 1–4, is a sectarian-minded party spirit: 'Each one of you saith, "I am of Paul", "and I of Apollos", "and I of Cephas".'[1] There is no question, at least in these four chapters, of formal heresy and false doctrine, for the names Paul, Apollos, Cephas are all beyond reproach. Nor is there any question of ecclesiastical schism, for he speaks later of the one Spirit bestowing on them diverse gifts,[2] of the one Baptism into one body,[3] and of the 'one bread, one body' of their Eucharist. It is

---

[1] I Cor. 1.12. I take it that there should be a full stop before the following words 'and I of Christ', and that these are St Paul's own words; he means to say 'I refuse to be tied up with any party. Is Christ divided?' etc. It is possible, however, that the words mean that there was a 'Christ-party', which took pride in being a "non-party party".'
[2] I Cor. 12.11.   [3] I Cor. 12.13.

true that the 'divisions' (*schismata*)[1] are apparent also at their Eucharist;[2] but as there plainly was one common meal, it seems likely that the different groups sat at separate tables, in different parts of the room. But it is clear that there was much to make St Paul very anxious in the existence of these groups, each with its favourite preacher, and at loggerheads with the others.

At 1.13 he starts at once with the Ground of Unity. Let me paraphrase freely: '*Christ* is not divided, even if you are. *Christ* was crucified for you. In *Christ's* Name you were baptized. Thank God none of you, or only very few of you, were baptized by me, for at least there is not the danger of "baptism by the hands of Paul" becoming a party-slogan! The Ground of Unity is the Gospel of God, Christ crucified for our salvation.'[3]

'Think of this Gospel of the Cross, which to the unbelieving world seems foolishness and nonsense. To the Jew it is a stumbling-block,[4] for he wants a Messiah to lead nationalist Judaism to victory over its Roman oppressors; and the very idea of a Messiah crucified by the hated Romans over whom He ought to have triumphed, is the denial of all his hopes. To the Greek the Gospel of the Cross seems sheer nonsense: he says, "You Christians tell us of a Jewish Messiah, doubtless an agitator who was very properly crucified by our Government, and you expect us to see in such a person a divine Saviour!" There is still to be seen on a wall in the ruins of the Palatine palace at Rome a rough sketch scratched in the plaster, of a crucified figure with an ass's head, and at the side a Christian lifting up his hands in worship, with the inscription 'Alexamenos worships his god'.

St Paul pursues his theme. 'God's wisdom, God's mighty and wonderful work for man's salvation, is foolishness in the eyes of the Greek, who is always fond of arguing and putting up clever speculations.[5] But the "foolishness" of God is wiser than men, and the "weakness" of God is stronger than men.[6] At Corinth,

[1] I Cor. 1.10. [2] I Cor. 11.18. [3] I Cor. 1.13–17. [4] I Cor. 1.23.
[5] I Cor. 1.20–1. [6] I Cor. 1.25.

look at the people whom He has chosen for the inestimable privilege of becoming His sons—people like you! Not many of you are noble, well-born, or powerful; you are "the weak things of the world", "things that are not", for in the eyes of the aristocracy of Corinth you simply do not exist. Yet it is you that He has chosen to manifest His glory in this place.[1]

'And so, when I Paul came to Corinth, I did not give you any of the Natural Theology which I preached with so little result at Athens; I was with you "in weakness and fear and in much trembling", anxious above all not to put up to you highsounding clevernesses of my own. They might have gone down only too well! No, it had to be "Jesus Christ and Him crucified"; the faith of the Church of God at Corinth must stand only on the mighty works of God and the present power of the Holy Spirit.'[2]

Then, after a brief digression on Christian Theology, to show that the Gospel is the very opposite of being intellectually contemptible, but is the highest wisdom,[3] he returns to the point of their divisions. 'Your party-spirit belongs to "the flesh": in other words, it reflects the attitude of fallen human nature, proud and self-opinionated. The very idea of putting Paul and Apollos on pedestals, as if we were rival Leaders of Thought!'[4] What is Paul, and what is Apollos? Simply ministers, servants, of the Lord, doing His work, proclaiming His Gospel, 'each as the Lord gave to him'. We are gardeners in His garden, builders of His Temple. The Temple is the Church [not of course the church-building, for none such existed]; the Christians themselves are the Temple, and they collectively form a Sanctuary in which the Presence of the Holy Spirit dwells.[5] As for Paul and Apollos, we are subject to God's judgment on the work that we do. If it is good and honest building, it will stand in the Day of the Judgment; if it is shoddy work, we shall have to answer for it.[6]

'The Church is God's building; its foundation is the foundation that God has laid, namely Jesus Christ.[7] It is not built on

[1] I Cor. 1.26–31.   [2] I Cor. 2.1–5.   [3] I Cor. 2.6–16.
[4] I Cor. 3.1–4.   [5] I Cor. 3. 16–17.   [6] I Cor. 3. 12–15.
[7] I Cor. 3.11.

human wisdom and cleverness; no one can rightly see his own place in it unless he sees himself as a fool and as a sinner; for only when he has learnt the truth about himself will he get things in the right proportion, and come to marvel at the infinite prodigality of the divine Love which has freely given to man *everything*. "For all things are yours, whether Paul, or Apollos, or Cephas, or the world, or life, or death, or things present, or things to come. All are yours, and ye are Christ's, and Christ is God's".[1]

Thus he sets in sharpest contrast the Word of God and the words of men. On the one side, the Word of the Gospel, God's supreme wisdom, the Cross, the gift of God to man in baptism, the Church as God's Temple. On the other side, the unspeakable folly of men who in the pride of their own wisdom reject this Gospel. And then, on the one side the words of men standing in right relation to God, whether it be as Apostles proclaiming God's Gospel and seeing themselves as subject to God's judgment on their work, or as simple believers, seeing their own littleness and praising God for His salvation. On the other side, the folly of men who lose sight of the Foundation and in their pride set up their own party-views and notions, and form cliques and sects.

I will now try to sum up the points which emerge from this.

(i) There is *the Unity which God has made*. Christ is not divided, even if men are. He died on the Cross for the salvation of sinners; in St John's words, 'that He might gather together in one the children of God which were scattered abroad'.[2] And as 'the weakness of God', shown in Christ's death by crucifixion, 'is stronger than men', so the Unity which God has made for men is one that human sin is not able to break. The Love of God is stronger: He has reconciled men with Himself, and thereby reconciled them with one another. The Unity which God has made does not depend on our faith or our faithfulness; it has been set up in spite of our sins. Christ is the Ground of Unity, the Foundation-stone which God has laid.

[1] I Cor. 3.18–23.   [2] John 11.52.

(ii) *The Visible Church is part of the Gospel.* Nothing could be plainer than this in Holy Scripture. From the beginning, the Purpose of God for man's salvation has been worked out through the believing and worshipping community, Israel the People of God; this was the first point which we had to notice in Chapter III. The Hebrew *qahal* is ordinarily translated in the Greek Bible as *ecclesia*, and so St Stephen speaks of 'the Church in the wilderness'[1] in the days of Moses. Thus the Bible was the Book of the Church, since within the Church all the books of the Bible were written, and within it our Lord was born. The Church of the New Testament is Israel as re-constituted by the Messiah, re-created by His death and resurrection, and enlarged to include the Gentile as well as the Jew. When St Peter at Pentecost calls the people to 'repent and be baptized',[2] he is calling them to come within the re-constituted Israel of God; Baptism and Eucharist have always been the two primary sacraments of initiation into and of life within this People of God.

Nothing is more plain in Holy Scripture than that under both covenants the Israel of God consists of sinful members who are the objects of God's mercy. Israel in the wilderness sins and murmurs and rebels again and again, and this is repeated continually throughout the history. In the New Testament, we need only recall the sins of the Corinthians; and we see the same happening through all church history. Man is continually sinning and receiving God's forgiveness and deliverance from sin's guilt and power; and this process will go on till the Last Advent of our Lord and the coming of His everlasting Kingdom, when the final victory will have been achieved *in* man, which was won *for* man by His precious death.

(iii) *Within this Unity various teachers have their place;* Paul, Apollos, Cephas, owning one Lord and proclaiming one Gospel, but doing so with different emphases, 'each as the Lord gave to him'. Within the Unity there is place for divers human opinions, interpretations, explanations, party-views; Paul, Apollos and Cephas know their place within the Unity as servants

---

[1] Acts 7.38.   [2] Acts 2.38.

of the Lord, as gardeners, as builders; they never allow their personal opinions to usurp the central place which belongs to the Gospel itself, to 'the fundamentals', mediated as they are by the Scriptures, the tradition of the Faith, the word preached, the sacraments, and the existence and structure of the Church itself. To these fundamentals no teacher, no party, no local church, no denomination, is allowed to add anything as necessary for salvation.

Thus is was right that within the Church of God at Corinth there should be Jewish and Gentile members, having their respective gifts to give, moral strictness on the one side, the freedom of the Spirit on the other; in danger of falling into legalism on the one side, antinomianism on the other; but able to help one another, as fellow-members of one body, as St Paul shows in I Cor. 12. Similarly there were in the Church of the fathers, the Antiochene and the Alexandrian schools of biblical interpretation; in the Latin Church of the middle ages and since, the diverse traditions represented by Benedictine, Dominican, Franciscan, Jesuit. Among the Reformers, there were the diverse insights of Luther and of Calvin; and so on. Yet again, there have been and are to-day the diverse gifts of the various nations and races; the northern European and the southern European, the Asians and the Africans. There are the diversities of European and American culture, and those of the nations which have turned communist; the diversity of capital and labour; of the intellectual, of the city-worker, of the countryman; and so on.

Within the whole catholicity of the Church of God all these have their place. For us, in our present condition of disintegration and division both in our social, economic and political life, and in our church life, this catholicity is very far from being realized. But it stands nevertheless as the God-given pattern. 'There is neither Jew nor Greek, there is neither bond nor free, there is neither male nor female; for ye are all one man in Christ Jesus'.[1] When St Paul wrote these words, he was very conscious that the diversities of race and social status and sex

[1] Gal. 3.28.

were still there; but he saw them all gathered into unity and the enmity taken away, within the Unity which God had made for mankind in Christ. If we believe with him that God was in Christ reconciling the world to Himself,[1] we are bound to hold to this pattern of unity.

(iv) *Disunion and disintegration are the fruits of the sectarian spirit* such as St Paul saw beginning to show itself in the little Corinthian church. While Paul, Apollos and Cephas understood their right place within the Unity, their self-styled adherents did not. They were going gravely and dangerously wrong, in regarding their own party-emphasis as complete and self-sufficient in itself, and allowing it to usurp the place which belonged to the Gospel of God.

The evil of party-spirit comes in whenever a party regards itself as self-sufficient and thinks that it possesses all the truth; it is right, the others are wrong. This is the sectarian spirit. It is possible for a party, while sacramentally in communion with another party in the Church, to lack any real spiritual contact with it. Thus it is possible for a party to become a 'denomination', when the ecclesiastical bond is broken.[2] For denominations to be called 'churches', as is now our habit, is of course completely unwarranted by the biblical use of the words 'church' and 'churches'.

Wherever there is this sectarian spirit in anything approaching an extreme form, something else is being added to the Ground of Unity; it is no longer simply the Gospel of God (with, of course, those necessary things that go with it: Bible, creed, Baptism, Eucharist, the existence of the Church and its structure), but the Gospel *plus* something else chosen by men and characteristic of the party view.

And so, says the accuser, those who are called Fundamentalists behave as a party, and treat the Ground of Unity not the Gospel of God but the Gospel *plus* the Inerrancy of the Bible and the necessity of a particular kind of Conversion.

[1] II Cor. 5.19.
[2] For this, see H. H. Kelly, *Catholicity*, S.C.M., 1932, esp. pp. 62–84.

At this point it is necessary for our discussion to take the dialogue-form of which I spoke in Chapter I. Since it is not as helpful to confess the sins of other people as it is to confess our own, it must at once be added that this is the common temptation of us all in our divided Christendom. So I begin by saying that the accuser says of us Anglicans, especially Catholic Anglicans, that we proclaim the Gospel of God *plus* Episcopacy and the Apostolic Succession.

Here it can rightly be protested that the accuser is less than fair; that the Catholic movement in Anglicanism is above all a religious movement, that in the emphasis which it throws on the sacraments it is emphasizing the objectivity of the Grace of God and finding protection from the perils of emotional religion; that it endeavours to integrate the common worship of the Church in the liturgy with all sorts of other things, with the age-long tradition of the Church, with the reading and the study of Scripture, with right reason applied to doctrine, with the Church's social duty, with the personal discipline of life, based on the call to an entire self-surrender to the will of God. It is within this complex that our insistence on Episcopacy has its place. But, true enough, there is the danger of being sectarian-minded, and emphasizing Episcopacy in such a way as to 'un-church' all those who have it not. We can and do fall into this danger. But, we say, it is not Episcopacy that is wrong. The right way for us is, that believing it to be a gift of God and directly related to the Gospel of God, we see in it something which in a re-integrated Christendom must become the possession of all Christians; so that now we who have it hold it in trust for those who have it not. St Augustine once said, apropos of the man in the gospel who said, 'Lord bid my brother that he divide the inheritance with me', that the right word in his controversy with the Donatists was, 'Lord, bid my brother that he *share* the inheritance with me.'

This last remark I owe to a Roman Catholic.[1] Of the Roman Catholic Church the accuser says that to the Gospel of God it

---

[1] Père Yves Congar, O.P., *Les chrétiens désunis*, Paris, 1937, p. 325. E.T. *Divided Christendom*, p. 260.

adds the demand for belief in the infallibility and the primacy of the Pope, with all else that marks Roman absolutism; that it habitually treats all other Christians as heretics and schismatics, claiming that it alone possesses the truth; that in all this it is mere sectarian-minded than any other denomination in Christendom. Perhaps one of the points where the Evil One succeeded in inflicting most grievous damage on the Church of God was that point in the early middle sixteenth century when the Roman authorities delayed and delayed to summon a Council while the situation was still fluid, till when the Council at last met at Trent the breach had become irreparable.[1]

But this is not the whole story. The Roman Church, though it seems to stand outside the ecumenical movement, is in fact deeply involved in it. Many signs of this might be cited; here is one. Ten years ago a French priest made public the fact that since his ordination he had been accustomed to say mass on St Bartholomew's day, the anniversary of the Huguenot massacres, as an act of sorrow and reparation for the sins of Christians against one another, and particularly of Catholics against Protestants. This, and much more that followed it, amounted to something like a public expression of regret and penitence, which has changed the whole attitude of Protestants towards Catholics in France. The day will come when Infallibility will be interpreted not negatively but positively, as true and faithful witness to the fundamentals of the Faith, to the Gospel of God. Amen, so be it.

So we might go the rounds. There are those who say, 'I am of Luther', and we Lutherans alone among Christians hold the true evangelical faith; or 'I am of Calvin', or 'I am of Wesley'. The re-integration of divided Christendom to which we look forward will mean, not that these diverse traditions are lost and perish, but that they will all be found within the fulness of the Church's catholicity.

And so the 'Fundamentalists'. The accuser says that they add to the Gospel of God the dogmas of Biblical Inerrancy and of a special kind of Conversion; that they behave like a sect; that if

[1] See Norman Sykes, *The Crisis of the Reformation*, Bles, p. 99.

they have no Index of Prohibited Books they voluntarily make such an Index by confining their reading to the books, pamphlets and papers published by the I.V.F. and the Tyndale Press; that I.V.F. will not co-operate with S.C.M.; that an 'International Council of Christian Churches' has come into being as a sectarian rival of the World Council of Churches.

At this point I will try to state their rejoinder as I believe they would state it. They will say: 'We have been assailed on every side, especially since the *Times* correspondence, by critics who in nearly every case fail to see what our movement in fact is. We regard this movement to which we belong as a mighty work of God in our day, not through any merit or worthiness on the part of those who are in it, but only through the action of God the Holy Spirit. There has been since the days of "The Fundamentals" a mighty revival of faith in Him, and countless souls have been brought to an entire personal surrender of themselves to God. The churches are to a large extent half-dead, not responsive to the living voice of God; most of us, having been brought up in them, have known what was literally a passing from death to life, by His personal life-giving touch.' C. T. Studd wrote from the heart of Africa in 1913: 'Before the whole world, and before the sleepy, lukewarm and namby-pamby Christian world, we will dare to trust our God, we will venture our all for HIM, we will live and we will die for HIM, and we will do it with His joy unspeakable singing aloud in our hearts. We will a thousand times sooner die trusting in our Lord than live trusting in men.'[1]

They might continue: 'This interdenominational missionary work has been given the name of "Faith Missions". There are the great denominational missions, whose "financial structure has been on the simple basis of a fixed rate of salary, an annual estimate of expenditure, and activities generally up to the limit of their budget. When they found that they had reached that limit they ceased to advance." Our way has been to keep our activities free from financial anxiety, and at missionary meetings

[1] Reproduced in facsimile in Norman Grubb, *After C.T. Studd; Sequel to the life of the famous pioneer-missionary*, R.T.S. and Lutterworth Press, 1939, opp. p. 16.

"to get our audiences rightly adjusted to God, to bring spiritual vision and sense of responsibility to them, leaving it to the Holy Spirit to move individuals to pray, work, give or go." "If the mission programme is based on God's invisible resources, then new projects and advances will be continually undertaken on the basis of an inexhaustible supply".'[1]

Here I will quote again from the Anglican letter from which I quoted before:[2] The Fundamentalists, 'by hanging on as they did to the simple, central, fundamental truths, of Divine guidance, of Divine supply for all needs, of Divine intervention of miracle, etc., when Liberal Theology was shaking faith in these things to their foundations, have kept the tradition of "free prayer" alive, when it has vanished almost completely, in my experience, from Liberal Protestant circles. For this I think we cannot be grateful enough.'

This 'free prayer' is the regular method of prayer in these missionary circles. There is a charming description from C. T. Studd's life, of a day in Africa when he was feeling seriously unwell, and stayed in bed past the time of the ordinary morning service. Some Africans, seeing him in bed on the verandah, came and chatted with him, till he began to wonder how he would be able to get out of bed and dress. 'Suddenly, to my consternation, I found the whole six kneeling round my bed, one after another letting out his heart in prayer for me. When the six had prayed, and before I could have my innings, the leader had pronounced the benediction, and a funny one it was, too! . . . These were by no means "classy" Christians, but some of the "weaker brethren". . . . These six were rank, raw, and vicious heathen six months ago, yet here they were with loosened tongues able to pray unasked and impromptu, and without a book.'[3]

I want to put in a strong plea for us, especially those of the Catholic tradition, to go to school in our prayer-life with 'Fundamentalists' of this sort, and for them to go to school with us. As

[1] Grubb, *After C. T. Studd*, pp. 183, 184. I have made this quotation to summarize in brief the contents of the book.
[2] p. 100 above.
[3] N. Grubb, *C. T. Studd, Cricketer and Pioneer*, pp. 175–6.

things are, we are mostly strangers to one another, aloof and mutually critical; which is to say that both we and they are in this respect guilty of the wrong party-spirit. Yet we are bound to believe, both we and they, that *whatever* gifts of grace and whatever fruits of the Holy Spirit are manifest among Christians, are bestowed by our Ascended Lord, who 'when He ascended up on high . . . gave gifts unto men'. It is He who has given them these gifts. Woe unto us if we put them down as 'varieties of religious experience', and pass on. It is our Lord who for the accomplishing of His Purpose has called these people to be His servants and has given them His Holy Spirit. To say that they have received of His Holy Spirit is not to say that they are perfect, well-balanced, complete; it is to say that they belong to Him. It can well be that they have gone a good deal further in His service than most of us.

Therefore let the barriers which separate us be broken down. Let us meet together, for the sake of what we and they have to give and what we and they have to get. Till we thus meet, we do not know, except in a general way, what they have to give to us, though even the little that has been said in this book may give some idea of it. But we do know that our church life is dreadfully tongue-tied, respectable and conventional, and theirs manifestly is not. (Yet we too have had a Father Stanton and a Father Dolling.) Let them teach us how to open our hearts to the Lord in free vocal prayer, and show us something of the recklessness of the surrender of lives to God.

And then there is what they need to receive from us, or rather, from what we have received in our inherited tradition. Do not they themselves feel the need of stability which is the fruit of long experience, in regard to the tradition of doctrine and of ways of worship, and of the ways of the spiritual life, as these can be learnt from the writings of the saints? or again, the importance of sacramental worship as witnessing to the objectivity of the Grace of God, to make it plain that it is by His Grace that we are saved, not by our efforts or our feelings, and not to check the freedom of the Spirit, but to regulate and guide it?

And then another point. The study of the long ages of church history brings to light many things in the past that throw light on the present, both for warning and encouragement. Here is one instance. It seems that in evangelical missions as a whole there has been a failure, as a rule, to deal wisely with heathen religious rites and customs, such as circumcision and practices relating to marriage; the tendency has been to sweep these away, as belonging to heathen darkness. The result is that they continue to be practised, unknown to the missionaries, or again that they reappear in new forms, especially when the native churches are free of European control, and lack the steadying influence of long Christian experience. On the whole, it seems that missions of the Catholic type are wiser in appreciating the fact that there exists a native culture which needs to be re-created and transformed; and this, partly because missions of this type are more aware of the Church's tradition, and partly because their sacramental worship itself has a cultural frame-work, with its rites and its calendar of festivals and fasts.

Further, with regard especially to the situation at home as well as in the missions, we have seen how many of those who are 'converted' are emotionally unstable, and immature and un-aware of the difficulties that lie ahead of them. We have seen, especially in the narrative from the Swedish book, something of the danger of the notion that it is possible for a converted person to live a life without sin; and that the only way of safety for him is to know that he is a sinner, and not to trust in his own efforts to live a holy life, but to know his own weakness and his constant need for the forgiveness of his sins. For lack of this, many 'converted' persons fall into serious moral trouble and psychological disorder. It is not for nothing that the Church, in her traditional forms of prayer, provides liturgical confession of sins, and provides the ministry of absolution.

Finally, there is the biblical doctrine of the Visible Church, which was completely missed both by Liberal Theology and by that of the older evangelicals, and consequently in the inter-denominational missions. But the Bible in both Testaments shows in the plainest way that the Israel of God is a visible com-munity, composed of sinful and fallible men, who are at the same time the objects of God's mercy. Even the saints of the Old Covenant, Abraham, Moses, David, Isaiah, are shown to be sinners.[1] In the New Testament, the traditions recorded in the gospels, which are derived from the Apostles themselves, tell of their sinfulness and indeed emphasize it strongly. But if any man sin, we have an Advocate with the Father, Jesus Christ the Righteous; and He is the propitiation for our sins.

[1] Gen. 20.1–13; Num. 20.1–12; II Sam. 11, 12; Isa. 6.5.

X

Faith in God

(i) *In form of servant*

WHAT does faith in God mean for us now, in the midst of this modern world which has become so deeply secularized? Must we hold aloof from the world, like Israel in the period after Ezra, that we may guard the integrity of the Faith and of the way of Christian living? Or must we say that, though fallen, it is still God's world, and find out how God is to be glorified in it?

Dr A. M. Ramsey, now Archbishop of York, gave a notable and important address entitled 'Faith and Society' to the Church Union School of Sociology, 1955.[1] In the course of the address, he sketched out the danger, common to all who live by the Bible, of making an enclave within the world, in which God might be truly glorified, and not facing the actual difficulties of living in the midst of the world; it must be remembered that his audience would be aware of this danger. It is to say that 'the Church is the redeemed community comprised of redeemed men and women and children. It is Christ's new creation; its life is already the life of the world to come. Ontologically, its members are re-born. Sociologically, they have fellowship with the Father and the Son through the indwelling of the Holy Spirit, and no secular concept of fellowship means the same thing. Morally, they are able to fulfil the hardest of Christ's commandments because His grace enables them to do so. They can turn the other cheek, abandon their goods in a vocation to poverty, or retain their wealth and (only just) be safe in its possession; they can follow a vocation to celibacy or carry out the marriage vow, as the heathen cannot be expected to who lack the grace that is

---

[1] Printed in the *Church Quarterly Review*, Oct.–Dec. 1955, pp. 360–6.

within the Church. Here is a realm in which Christian sociology is possible, an island-realm amid the perishing world. But do not expect such possibilities in the world that lieth in the evil one. Any moral impact the Church may have upon the world is in God's hands and cannot be made the subject of theory. Furthermore, expect that any approximations to God's Kingdom from the side of the world may be bogus and misleading, because pride and titanism infect such efforts and bring them to grief.'[1]

This is expressed in a 'Catholic' idiom; Evangelicals would put it quite differently. But many Evangelicals would themselves agree with the substance of the statement, and would add some words about the duty of evangelism at home and abroad in order to bring as many people as possible to the saving knowledge of Christ. Their emphasis here would be a religious emphasis, on the call to men to give their lives to Christ. But would they be able to say what men are to do with their lives after they have done so, in their business, commerce or industry, beyond the guarding of their own personal integrity? It is with this problem of daily life in the midst of the world that Dr Ramsey is grappling in this address.

The problem here is one that goes to the root of the meaning of the Incarnation of the Son of God. Let us go back to the great statement of it in Phil. 2.6–11, of which I will quote a paraphrase: '*Have this mind in you which is yours in Christ Jesus, who, being in the form of God*, that is, being in his essential nature God, *thought it not a thing to be grasped at, to be on an equality with God*. The word is *robbery* in the Authorized Version and *prize* in the Revised Version. It means, rather, a thing to be snatched or clung on to. Unlike the first Adam who, having no right to be on an equality with God, grasped at it, the second Adam, having every right, did not assert his right but *emptied himself, taking the form of servant, being made in the likeness of men, and being found in fashion as a man humbled himself, becoming obedient*. What did it mean to become obedient, being found in fashion as a man? It

[1] Ibid., pp. 362–3.

meant accepting all the conditions of humanity as it were at their face value.'[1]

The Son of God emptied Himself of His heavenly glory that He might manifest that glory 'in the form of servant', under conditions of actual human life, and in contact with men. In His ministry He went among non-churchgoing people, and shared their meals and their drinks, knowing that He would be reviled by the more respectable sort as 'a gluttonous man and a winebibber, a friend of publicans and sinners'. The Pharisees would have been only too glad to see such people repent of their evil lives, turn over a new leaf, and attend synagogue; while they were among them, they would have been conscious all the time that they were good-living people, and these others were not. But our Lord was different. Those people did not feel that He was 'coming down to their level', but that He *was* somehow on their level. He 'knew what was in man'; He was interested in them as persons, cared about them and their affairs, invited their confidences. He did not inwardly despise them; He was their friend. He did indeed bring them to repentance, but a repentance that was more than a mere moral amendment; He showed to them God.

The godly were for Him a far harder problem. He found in them a consciousness of their own virtue, deeply rooted in self-love and spiritual pride, and strongly armoured against anything that might wound their self-esteem. Yet to them also He had been sent, to them most of all as the spiritual leaders of Israel. For He had come to Israel as her Bridegroom, according to the figure which had appeared first in the prophecy of Hosea, as an image of the union of Israel with the Lord her God. So our Lord had come to be united with Israel His People, that she might become in truth the People of God. But as in the days of Hosea, so now, Israel was 'a faithless and adulterous generation'.[2] Yet she was still Israel, the Bride; the union could not be broken by divorce. Therefore He must bear her sins, even if in her faithlessness she brought Him to the death of the cross.

[1] T. R. Milford, in *This Mind in You*, addresses to clergy, 1949, privately printed.
[2] Mark 8.38; Matt. 12.39; 16.4.

The condition of the Incarnation was that He should not move about among us men as a sort of Superman, omniscient and possessing complete information about everything, omnipotent and able to work all manner of marvels at will; for that would mean that He still retained His heavenly glory, covered with a thin veil. This is a form of the Monophysite heresy, to which reference has been made earlier. The condition of the Incarnation was that of true manhood: He was made one with is in all the 'fashion' (*schēma*, the outward shape) of our human life, bearing the form (*morphē*, the essential nature) of servant; made like unto us in all things, yet without sin.[1]

Such is also the condition of the Church's life in this world; it too bears 'the form of servant'. It will not always be so; we look in hope to our Lord's everlasting Kingdom, when He who on earth bore the form of a servant will be manifested in divine glory as King, seated with the Father on His throne, and the Church, redeemed mankind, will share in that glory. But now on earth the Church is as He was; her members are to minister as He ministered, and to identify themselves in love with their fellow-men, as He did.

Our temptation is to follow the way of the first Adam, who sought to snatch at heavenly glory, by seeking to live now on earth as if the Last Advent of our Lord had already happened; to withdraw from the world and live in an island-realm apart. This withdrawal is what Dr Sasse,[2] meant by a *theologia gloriae*— seeking to live with our Lord in the continual light of His Presence, and leaving the world to live in darkness under the power of the evil one. Fridfeldt in our Swedish story was trying to do this. But he pointed out the better way in his sermon: the forgiven sinner '*always* desires to be and *sometimes* is able to be humble like Jesus, patient like Jesus, obedient like Jesus'.[3] This way is that of the *theologia crucis*, which means the acceptance of the form of servant and of identification with men, and involves seeing ourselves as fellow-sinners with them.

This true way of obedience means that our life is to be lived in two worlds at once, as citizens of the heavenly city, a 'colony of

[1] Heb. 4.15.   [2] p. 59 above.   [3] p. 114 above.

heaven'[1] in this world, and knowing in our worship and prayer
our heavenly inheritance; and *at the same time* to be identified
with our fellow-men—going through military training, accepting the responsibilities of an employer of labour, and of direct-
ing some great industrial concern, or working as an employee
in the factory, or an office-worker rubbing shoulders with the
office-staff, or as a farmer on the land, or as a mother bringing
up children. All these are ways of vocation, in which man is
called to glorify God by the way in which he does his work and
by the life which he lives with his fellow-men. Every situation in
which the Christian finds himself is a situation in which God is
to be glorified, by His will being done.

It is wrong, therefore, to think of the work of the Christian
Ministry, in some form, as the only way of serving God; to
think that we are only serving Christ when we are winning
souls to Him: to think that a man is serving Christ when he is
teaching in Sunday-school and not when he is attending a
trades-union meeting. The ordained minister and the lay-
evangelist have indeed the most important task of all; but to say
that they alone are truly serving God is to deny that the world
is God's world. In fact their duty is to be servants of God's
people by interpreting to them the meaning of their various
vocations, by helping them to see how God is to be glorified in
the office or the factory, and by helping them through the difficulties which beset them in this world which, though it is God's
world, is a fallen world.

(ii) *Idolatry*

The words with which St John ends his first epistle, 'Little
children, keep yourselves from idols', are words of deep significance and importance. The word 'idol' does not mean only
the graven or molten images of his god which the heathen
makes, images which are made to represent God but which are
not God. It stands for anything which a man worships instead
of God, anything which a man makes or finds for himself to

---

[1] Moffatt's rendering of Phil. 3.20.

spend his life for it. For Christians, it means especially any kind of representation of God which we men proceed to treat as if it were God, and put faith in it instead of in Him. Let us see how this works out.

Covetousness, says St Paul, is idolatry.[1] Idolatry it is, when men devote their lives to making money, for the sake of what money will buy: comforts and luxuries, a social position, power over other men's lives. The pursuit of wealth can dominate a man's life, absorb his energies, fill his imagination; it can become the thing that he lives for, and in all but name the god that he worships. Here as in all forms of idolatry it is ultimately the Self which is setting itself up as the final object of worship, in place of God the true object of worship. But I want to reflect first on the way in which idolatry affects *me*.

If I were writing a book of Confessions, I might write something like this: I am a person who writes books from time to time; and authorship is a work of self-expression, like that of an artist or a poet; and all self-expression is delightful, if laborious. I like expressing my ideas, my favourite ways of putting things, and what I regard as my 'insights'. It may be that these ideas are excellent ideas, in my own estimation if not in that of others; but these ideas, in proportion to their real or imagined excellence, can become an idol; they can become a substitute for faith in God, and effectually debar me from real faith in Him. Someone has said—I think Thomas a Kempis—'If you want to know and learn something usefully, love to be unknown and to be accounted for nothing'. The beginning of any knowledge of reality is to see my own littleness in the sight of God; and if I am saying in my heart, with reference to the aforesaid beautiful ideas, 'God, I thank thee that I am not as other men are', I am committing idolatry. I am putting something which I have made in place of God, and admiring it instead of worshipping Him. I need to get a right perspective. It is not that my ideas need necessarily be scrapped. But I must see how inadequate they must needs be, in comparison with Him of whom they are representations.

[1] Col. 3.5; cf. Eph. 5.5.

The peril of idolatry comes very near to everyone, just because the supreme peril of every soul is the love of the Self. There can be a personal and private idolatry; and there can be a corporate idolatry of the group or party or sect or denomination. The sectarian spirit itself, of which something was said in the chapter before this, rests on a form of idolatry. A sect, as was said there, does not accept the Gospel of God as it is, with the necessary *media* through which it is set forth, but the Gospel of God *plus* something else. In the case of parties and sects in the Church of God, this something else will always be one of the things which have their right place in the economy of the Church of God, but now falsified by becoming the badge of the sect which attaches to it an interpretation of its own.

I must give some instances. The accuser says of 'Catholic' Christians generally, that we commit idolatry in the worship of the Holy Sacrament of the Eucharist. So we do, if and when in our thought of the Sacrament or in our worship, we think of IT and not of HIM. But the Holy Sacrament is our Lord's own gift to us; when we celebrate it, we 'show the Lord's death till He come'.[1] It is an outward and visible sign, signifying a heavenly and spiritual reality; a sign pointing us to our Lord incarnate, crucified, risen and ascended, and a means whereby we are brought into contact with Him, and through which He acts, bestowing His grace. There will be no idolatry in so believing and worshipping, when in the visible sign or sacrament we worship our living and ascended Lord. But there can be and is idolatry if we think of 'it' as efficacious, apart from Him. There can be such idolatry among Protestants if they come to Communion in the hope that 'it' will 'do them good' and make them feel devout; just as there can be idolatry among Catholics if they offer the sacrifice of the Mass in the hope that 'it' will win for them some desired petition.

Again, with regard to Papal Infallibility, the accuser says that this is something added to the Gospel of God, which takes away from the authority of the Word of God spoken in the

[1] I Cor. 11.26.

Bible. There can be idolatry here, if the voice of the chief bishop of the visible Church is identified with the Voice of God. But there will be no idolatry if the two are distinguished, and the Pope is seen simply as witnessing to the revelation of God set forth once and for all in the Bible.

As there can be idolatry of the eucharistic sacrament and of the Church, so there can be Bibliolatry, Idolatry of the Bible. It was the habitual sin of the Jewish rabbis to identify the Word of God with the revelation of His Word in the five books of the Law, and thereby to make the written word a substitute for God. The Law had been given them that through it they might know Him; they were tempted to make the knowledge of the written word a substitute for the knowledge of Him, and to make the scrupulous observance of the Law a substitute for the real service of Him. So our Lord says to them,[1] 'Ye search the Scriptures, for *in them* ye think that ye have eternal life . . . and ye will not *come to me* that ye may have life.'

There is the peril of Bibliolatry to-day, when the Word of God is simply identified with the written word of the Bible; the peril lurks in the demand that the Word of God should come to us uncontaminated by any human error. There can be idolatry when the Bible is taken in this way, much as it was said of the ex-tractarian Roman Catholic W. G. Ward that he would gladly have had a papal encyclical on his breakfast table every morning, to tell him exactly what he was to think and to do. For idolatry means, not worshipping the God who actually exists, but some substitute for Him which is to hand; God Himself is too big for us, so let us have a manageable God, a God brought down to our own level. There can be idolatry of the Bible, when it is used to provide ready-made answers to our problems, and save us from the need of comparing this particular text from the Bible with others, and thinking the matter out.

But there will be no idolatry when the Bible is not treated thus as an oracle, when the written word is not simply identified with the Voice of God, when the necessary distinction is made between God's own Word and the words of men through which

[1] John 5. 39–40.

His Word is spoken. When that distinction is made, it becomes possible to think that there can be errors, of some sort, in the human words, provided that they are not such errors as would make the Bible no longer the Bible. And errors there are; there are the admitted imperfections of the Old Testament on the subjects of morality and law and of nationalism; but these are all made good when God is revealed in His Son, who is personally His Word. There are errors of fact; but they do not affect the essential truth of the record of the working out of God's Purpose for man's salvation. We are reminded here of what Professor Fuller said to us[1] about the 'condescension' of God in giving us His treasure in earthen vessels, in stooping to declare His Word through the words of fallible men, and of the way in which he linked this up with the true humanity of our Lord in the Incarnation. Our Lord's true humanity, he said, is denied by the Monophysite heresy. Now we see that Monophysitism involves a kind of idolatry, in not accepting the revelation of God in Christ as it is given to us, but putting up a substitute of our own instead.

But the danger of an idolatry of the Bible is near and present. It appears to be a special danger for young people who come under the influence of the Evangelical Unions; such for instance as medical students, who having been converted and having accepted the Bible as true, will not listen to the doctrine of Evolution as it is presented to them by their lecturers in their physiological studies. I am allowed to quote here some words of Sir John Wolfenden, who after many years as a schoolmaster and headmaster is now Vice-Chancellor of the University of Reading, on 'the Closed Mind'. The passage quoted came near the end of an address given to a conference of schoolmistresses at Oxford in the Christmas vacation of 1955-6:

'One more problem, and then I have done. Thirty-five years ago, when I was in a Sixth Form, there was a recognized and official conflict between Science and Religion. It went so deep that the two were normally recognized as being mutually exclusive—if you claimed to be a scientist that meant that you

[1] p. 77-8 above.

rejected religion, whereas if you professed any kind of religion you could never aspire to be a scientist. I am told that, at least in that extreme form, the conflict no longer exists. . . . But there is, I suspect, another form of the same disjunction which is current to-day. It is the antithesis between, on the one hand, the free and fearless ranging of the intellect and, on the other, a neo-obscurantism which takes its start from a literal-minded fundamentalism. I do not wish to give offence or to trouble impertinently the waters of anyone's religious faith. But I am frightened—that is not too strong a word—by the number of young people who to-day come from Sixth Forms to Universities with their minds firmly closed, locked, bolted and barred, not just about the Bible and religion in general, but about all sorts of other things as well, philosophy, politics and history among them. And I beg you all to beware lest in tenderness towards a naïve form of Christian belief we should be shutting the door on the Holy Spirit of Truth. There can, in the long run, be no conflict between different forms of truth. Religious truth and scientific truth may seem to conflict. But this can be no more than a superficial appearance, caused by our incompleteness of perception of the one or the other. Truth is one and indivisible, because God is one and indivisible. The Holy Spirit is not to be confined within the limits of our partial human comprehension. And if there appears to be a conflict, it is more humble, more modest, more scholarly and more Christian to suppose that we are at fault than that God is. The operations of the scientific intellect are no less a divinely-inspired activity than the simple beliefs of the immature young. Whatever else it is, education, for us and for our pupils, is an attempt, to be strenuously pursued with all the power we have, to find and follow the truth wherever we can find it. For the Holy Spirit is the Holy Spirit of Truth.'[1]

I continue with the newspaper report of the discussion: 'The

---

[1] This quotation is from the text of Sir John Wolfenden's address, which he very kindly sent me. The following paragraph is from the Adelaide *Advertiser*, 20th Jan. 1956, from which I came to know about the address; it gave a fairly full account of this part of the address, and further material which he tells me is taken from the discussion which followed. He has no notes of the discussion, but is prepared to endorse the remarks here attributed to him.

strong revival of what seemed to him (Sir John) to be a remarkably naïve form of Christian beliefs had two results. One was that it went deep into the young person; he or she tended at too early an age to come to a stop, fixed in that set of views and not wanting to enquire any further. That acceptance of an immature form of belief spread away from just a religious belief into all the other subjects, so that the early, premature acceptance of a fixed undeveloped set of ideas applied to other things as well. This meant that by the age of seventeen or eighteen the whole front of development was static. The second thing was that some of the young people who had this particular form of central belief expressed those beliefs in ways which anyone who had looked at the scientific and evolutionary approach to the subjects found ludicrous. It was very frightening, because it meant a lot of young people were being petrified in their whole mental development at the very moment when they ought to be becoming the opposite. . . . He had uttered some things once at a North London meeting which were evidently regarded as offensive. . . . He had said that he was rather shocked when he heard people talking about prayer as if it were the automatic demanding of something you wanted without any particular effort on your part. He had no use for the boy and girl at school who wasted two or three years and then went into examinations, shut their eyes and prayed.'

'Minds firmly closed, locked, bolted and barred'—with Sir John Wolfenden, I find it very frightening. I try to imagine what can be the train of thought, and I see it thus: 'I am converted—the Bible is true—those who are converted are children of light, those who are not are in the darkness—the world lieth in the evil one—the wisdom of this world is foolishness with God —my teachers appear to be in the darkness, for they put across to me the world's science which is contrary to the Bible.' There is need, surely, for someone who is in touch with the facts to write a special study of this alarming phenomenon. For it is another instance of idolatry, of not facing up to the real God who exists, and setting up a substitute for true faith in Him in the form of a set of beliefs which chime in with the conflict of the young against their elders, and with a shirking of the discipline which a school imposes.

This special study which I am asking for could well relate this menacing phenomenon in the religious sphere with other phenomena which have appeared in recent years: Fascism and Nazism, where 'the party' claimed the entire allegiance of its adherents, and proceeded, often by the methods of the gangsters, to gain control of the political machine; the similar phenomenon of 'the party' among the Communists, as when after World War II they gained control in Czechoslovakia, and similarly the Afrikaner party in South Africa and the McCarthy intrigues in the United States. The parliamentary system can be so manipulated as to overthrow the whole principle of democracy. This evil spirit is abroad everywhere; here in Australia the arrangement of the constituencies has been so manipulated by the parties which have been in power that in Queensland it is next to impossible for there to be any other than a Labour Government, and in South Australia that it is difficult for a Labour Government ever to attain to power. The schisms and divisions in our political and economic and social and international life are deeper and more serious than those which exist in the Church.

(iii) *Faith in God, in the midst of the modern world*

Real faith in God is faith in the real God, the God who exists. This faith is menaced on every side by the temptation to idolatry, which is the setting up of a man-made idol, of one sort or another, as a substitute for the real God. We have seen something of the variety of forms in which this idolatry can insinuate itself, and of the subtlety of the temptation of idolatry. Idolatry involves not only the dishonouring of God, but also the debasing of man who is made in God's image. It involves sometimes a manipulation of religion to further human ends, so that man does not truly worship God; it involves nearly always the subjection of the human person to a party, to party catchwords and propaganda; and it involves the abdication by man of the responsibility of forming his own judgment, in favour of the non-rational suggestions which are conveyed to him on every side, on the films, by the radio, novels, advertisements, and the like.

We must then consider first the important problem of Education. Sir John Wolfenden, as we have seen, is anxious about a species of propaganda which to a serious extent is making real education impossible. What is the purpose of studies—apart, of course from the acquisition of the necessary technical knowledge to equip the student for his life-work? The real purpose is above all to train his mind, so that he may be capable of forming an intelligent and responsible judgment, and of making honest criticisms, both in those matters with which he will have to deal professionally, and in his life as a citizen. He must know what words mean, and be able to use them correctly; he must see that words are vehicles of ideas, see that human notions and ideas, including his own, are imperfect and incomplete (he knows by experience how much he has learnt from others); and he must see that there is a truth of things, beyond and above his own ideas and those of others. This is to be an educated man; and our society can be in a healthy state only when it has a sufficiency of such men to lead it. The vice of the spirit of 'the party' is that it deliberately rejects this training up of a sound and responsible judgment, and seeks instead a conformity with the party aims and its propaganda.

Plainly there is a theological meaning in Education. God has made man in His own image, with a mind to think and a will to decide; these are to be used to His glory in His world. The Bible has much to say about the gift of Wisdom; Solomon is commended for seeking this gift,[1] with special reference to the responsibilities of a king. In Isa. 6.9-10 the prophet becomes aware that the people to whom he is sent have not eyes to see nor ears to hear; and this passage of Isaiah is echoed in our Lord's repeated exhortation, 'He that hath ears, let him hear', and 'Take heed what ye hear', or rather 'Look to see what it is that you are hearing', *blepete ti akouete*.[2] On Whitsunday we pray

[1] I Kings 3.　　　　　　　　[2] Mark 4.24.

for the gift of the Holy Spirit: 'grant us by the same Spirit to have a right judgment in all things'. 'All things' includes not only what we call spiritual things, but the questions which come up in social life, in politics, in judgments about poetry and art, in judgments about other people. If we are to have faith in God in the midst of this modern world, we must be seeking continually this gift of right judgment in all these things.

So for instance in political things, this gift of right judgment means the will and the ability to discern what is the right way, what is the way that is according to the truth, and distinguish this from the way that promises some immediate advantage for the church (denomination) to which we belong, or for our nation. It is to be feared that Christians to-day very commonly fall short of a right standard of judgment in regard to Communism, which is very plainly one of the great issues about which we of the West have to make up our minds. It is so plain that Communism denies most of the beliefs about God and man which we hold dear, that it becomes plausible and easy to regard Communism as the embodiment of all evil. But there are fellow-Christians of ours who live in Communist countries; what way should we desire to follow if we were in their shoes? This question illustrates in so interesting a way our problem of the way of faith in God in this modern world, that a word needs to be said about it.

There are places on the other side of the Iron Curtain where Christians are accepting the situation of living under a professedly atheistic government. They are reproached for it; why, it is asked, do they not denounce the regime, and 'go underground'? Are they not compromising with Communism? They say: Our situation is very different from that of the Christians in Germany under the Nazis. Hitler was prepared to favour Christianity, provided that it conformed to the Nazi ideology; he supported the so-called 'German Christians' under Reichsbischof Müller, who were determined to exclude all Jews from the Church. On this point the 'confessing Christians' were compelled to stand out and resist; the Nazis were prepared to tolerate Christianity only if it became heretical. But Communism has no such programme; it does not identify itself with any Christian heresy, for it rejects Christianity altogether. Therefore, they say, it is possible to live under it.

About Christianity, the Communists say two things: first, that it is a form of belief that rests on outworn superstitions and is supported by indefensible arguments, and second, that it is wholly tied up with bourgeois capitalism. There are some Christians there beyond the Iron Curtain, as there are in our own countries, who give every colour to these two imputations. But these Christians are demonstrating by their teaching and their life the falsity of them both. As regards the first, they give an honest statement of their belief in terms of present-day thought; indeed they can do no other, since all citizens are indoctrinated with Communist teaching, and students have to attend courses of lectures daily on the Hegelian and Marxist dialectic. They know what they are up against, and they counter this with the dialectic of the Cross and Resurrection of Christ. As regards the second, they prove that the Church is not bound up with bourgeois capitalism by living as loyal citizens under their government. Consequently they earn the respect of the Communists.

The following story was told us by one who was the chief actor in it, a prominent evangelical churchman who makes it his business to be on friendly terms with the political leaders, and has certainly won their respect. He told us that they had mentioned to him recently that a new law was soon to be introduced, the purport of which they described to him. He shook his head, and said that he and his people could not live under such a law. They replied that if this was really so, they must get the terms of the law altered. I was reminded of a story told me by our Father Herbert Kelly at Kelham, of a conversation with a Free Church S.C.M. leader whom he had known for a long time, and who said to him, 'Father, we agree with you more than you think'. Father Kelly replied, 'Yes, I know you do.' It seemed to me that the relation of Father Kelly with that Free Churchman was not unlike that of my friend with the Communist leaders. He was living among the Communists, holding fast to his Christian faith, and standing up to them when necessary. He was accepting the situation in which God had put him, and in that situation bearing his Christian witness.

He said to us that it made great demands on their fortitude to live as Christians in that Communist country, and yet they were serenely happy to be there. But he thought it would be more difficult to bear a vital Christian witness in a country such as Australia or Great Britain, countries which are nominally Christian, but in which all sorts of issues are confused and unclear. To use our terminology in this chapter, our Christianity is beclouded by many sorts of idolatry.

What is the meaning of Faith in God in the midst of this modern world? It begins with personal belief and personal self-committal to our Lord. But when we have done this, or begun to do so, how do we go on to live our lives in the world? We are not doing our duty if we seek to contract out of the world; we must find out how God is to be glorified in the life of Christians in the world.

It is just here that conservative evangelicals and Fundamentalists need to take seriously and not merely resent criticisms such as this: that when 'the Gospel which proclaims God in His own right and calls for moral decision and submission' is preached by Fundamentalists, 'the mind of the hearer has either to be stifled or ignored on account of the crudity of the doctrine presented, and the appeal is made to *less than the whole man*. The act of decision and conversion, instead of being related to man's place and duty in society, abstracts a man from his place and duty in society, and society becomes the mere stage and scenery alongside which the moral decisions are made. The moral will is separated from its context, because the appeal is made to less than the whole man as a reasoning being and a social being.'[1]

I have been trying in this chapter to put a criticism such as this in its context, and show that it is far from being idle abuse. Needless to say, the mission of the Church to the modern world

[1] Dr A. M. Ramsey, in the paper already quoted; *Church Quarterly Review*, Oct. 1955, p. 361–2.

poses a problem for us all; many valiant efforts are being made in many different quarters to tackle it, but the need is far from being met.

The mission of the Church to our modern world is that men and women of faith should by their intercession and in their lives take their place among the toiling multitudes who bear the burden and heat of the day in doing the world's work: manual workers and office workers; those who work on railways, buses, planes, those who go to sea; those who bear responsibilities of organizing and controlling labour; doctors and all who minister to the sick; all who work on the land— that in these and all the other ways of life there should be active Christians sharing the job with them, and putting into practice the truth that every honourable way of life is a vocation, in which God is to be glorified. There are multitudes who have difficulties of belief; and here it is not a matter merely of answering their questions, but still more of asking with them the questions; not merely of providing a human solution, but of helping them through all their difficulties to the Answer which is in Christ alone. As our Lord came not to be ministered unto but to minister, so must we His servants. As the way that He followed led Him to the Cross, in giving His life as ransom for many, so for us, the way of faith in God in the midst of this modern world means not only to receive the redemption with which He has bought us, but also to bear the cross after Him, in taking our place side by side with our suffering fellow-men, and sharing their burdens. We are not to stand on the shore and let them do the toiling; we are to share it with them. For He took on Himself 'the Form of a Servant.'

Postscript

THREE things have specially impressed themselves upon me in the writing of this book.

The first has been the splendid emphasis which those whom the world calls Fundamentalists lay on the fundamentals of the faith. St Paul wrote, 'I am not ashamed of the Gospel; for it is the power of God unto salvation to every one that believeth; to the Jew first, and also to the Greek'.[1] In them these words come alive, in their belief in the Gospel, in their acceptance of the authority of the Gospel for themselves and for their fellow-men, and therefore in their evangelism both in the home lands and in the missions abroad. No criticisms of 'the Fundamentalists' can meet with anything but justified resentment where this is not understood.

The second is the manner in which the inadequacy of the doctrine of the Inerrancy of Scripture has demonstrated itself. It is too narrow to fit the facts; it cannot be carried through in the exegesis of Scripture without resort to special pleading; it does not explain the admitted imperfection of the Old Testament; it involves a materialistic notion of Truth. Above all, in being a negative word, it is quite inadequate to express the glory of the revelation of God in the Scriptures.

The third is, the wonder of the truth that the visible Church of God is composed of sinners. It is presupposed in every part of the Scriptures; the notion that the True Church in this world is composed of converted people only, living sinless lives, is quite alien to the Scriptures. The Swedish preacher was right when he spoke of 'Jesus only' and thought of the Cross as set up on high over a world of tempted and sinful men, bringing forgiveness for all who repent, and repentance for all who believe.

Here is the Ground of Christian Unity. The Church and the world are full of parties, sects, divisions, and Fundamentalism

[1] Rom. 1.16.

148

is one of them. But there is a Unity which God has made, and the only way of salvation for any of us is to be within that Unity, to be 'in Christ'. This demands of us that we bear with one another, bear with people who are blind in heart and troublesome and difficult, bear with Bible critics and with worldly-minded people and unbelievers, bear their burdens with them and for them, that they may be helped to find peace in Him. The only safe way for us in this world is the Way of the Holy Cross; the only right theology for us in this world is *theologia crucis*. *Theologia gloriae* is for the World to Come, when our Lord shall have come again.

An Index

An Index

Mainly of Subjects